Chloe's Vegan Desserts

Chloe's Vegan Desserts

More than 100 Exciting New Recipes for Cookies and Pies, Tarts and Cobblers, Cupcakes and Cakes—and More!

Chloe Coscarelli

ATRIA PAPERBACK

New York   London   Toronto   Sydney   New Delhi

ATRIA PAPERBACK

A Division of Simon & Schuster, Inc.
1230 Avenue of the Americas
New York, NY 10020

First Atria paperback edition February 2013

ATRIA PAPERBACK and colophon are trademarks of Simon & Schuster, Inc.

For information about special discounts for bulk purchases,
please contact Simon & Schuster Special Sales
at 1-866-506-1949 or business@simonandschuster.com.

The Simon & Schuster Speakers Bureau can bring authors to your live event. For more information or to book an event,
contact the Simon & Schuster Speakers Bureau at 1-866-248-3049 or visit our website at www.simonspeakers.com.

DESIGNED BY ERICH HOBBING

Manufactured in the United States of America

10   9   8   7   6   5   4   3   2   1

Library of Congress Cataloging-in-Publication Data

Coscarelli, Chloe.
  Chloe's vegan desserts : more than 100 exciting new recipes for cookies and pies, tarts and cobblers, cupcakes and cakes—
and more! / Chloe Coscarelli.
      p. cm
  Summary: "The first vegan winner of Cupcake Wars—and of any reality cooking show!—Chef Chloe, author of the popular
Chloe's Kitchen, brings her signature creativity and fun to the best part of every meal: Dessert! Chloe's fantastic-tasting,
beautiful desserts are what first got her national media attention when she wowed the judges on Food Network's Cupcake
Wars. And her famous desserts are what her enthusiastic fans always demand. Now Chef Chloe offers her first all-dessert
cookbook—and you will just not believe these delicious dishes are vegan. Instead of relying on the tofu, applesauce, egg
replacer, and mashed bananas that many other vegan cooks use, Chloe works a different kind of food science magic, with
liquid proportions and leaveners like baking soda and vinegar to make cakes rise and remain moist and to give her food a
texture and taste that vegans and non-vegans alike crave. Go ahead and lick that spoon! There're no worries when you cook
vegan. Chloe re-creates classic desserts and treats from creme brulee to tiramisu to beignets as well as store-bought favorites—
made with a humorous taste twist—like her ChloeO-type Oreos and Pumpkin Whoopie Pies. Chloe also serves up brand-new
triumphs like her dreamy Lemon Olive Oil Cake with Rosemary Ice Cream, Coconut and Chocolate Cream Pies, Coconut
Sorbet with Cashew Brittle, and a dozen innovative cupcake creations. Who can possibly resist? With 100 fabulous, easy-to-
make recipes and gorgeous color photography, Chloe's Vegan Desserts is the next great innovative baking and dessert book
with a universal appeal"—Provided by publisher.
  Includes index.
  Summary: "Over 100 original recipes for delicious and fun vegan desserts"—Provided by publisher.
  1. Desserts. 2. Vegan cooking. I. Title.
  TX773.C63445 2013
  641.86—dc23
            2012027147

ISBN 978-1-4516-3676-5
ISBN 978-1-4516-3677-2 (ebook)

To my mom,
the greatest baker,
who taught me that any dinner mishap
could be saved by a brilliant dessert.

Contents

Pies, Tarts, and Cobblers

Cakes and Cupcakes

Spoon Desserts

Drink Up!

Basics

Introduction

Dessert has always made my world go round. When I was in fourth grade, my teacher gave the class an assignment to write about our favorite sandwiches. While all the other kids wrote about ham, cheese, and PB&J, I wrote about ooey-gooey s'mores. In fact, it never even occurred to me to think savory, but I ended up getting an A+ for creativity!

If you've got a sweet tooth, you will agree that the only point of birthdays is birthday cake and that no meal is ever complete without dessert. I'm almost always covered in flour and my guilty pleasure is eating pure melted dark chocolate with a spoon. Sound familiar? Read on.

SWEET MISTAKES

Almost everyone has a baking-gone-wild story in their past. One of my first cookie-baking experiences as a child was a complete disaster, and I'm talking far worse than a burnt batch of cookies. A lock of my hair got caught in my electric stand mixer and pulled my head an inch away from the high-speed whisk. My brother Andy, the hero, pulled the plug just in time. Phew! I don't know what was more traumatic: the actual experience or walking around with a hideous melon-sized knot in my hair for the next month. The point is, if I could overcome this ultimate baking horror story and still face a stand mixer, anyone can! So, for those of you who think you can't bake, let go of forgetting-to-add-the-sugar or smoke-alarm-in-the-kitchen memories. Today you can unleash your inner pastry chef! Don't let the old adage that baking is an exact science scare you. Sure, you have to measure, but there's more leeway than you might think.

MY SECRET TO PERFECTION

Many years ago, my mom and I underbaked a batch of vegan brownies we were making for a party. They were still delicious, but way too soft in the center. My mom, being the brilliant hostess that she is, suggested we call them Chocolate Soufflé Squares instead. Our guests devoured them and to this day, have been begging us for our "secret" Chocolate Soufflé Square recipe. I guess the secret is out! Bottom line: If something goes wrong in the kitchen, simply change the name of the dessert. Did the pumpkin pie not set up properly? Call it pumpkin *pudding* pie. Did you leave the peanut butter cookies in the oven a bit too long? Call them peanut butter *crisps*. Get the hang of it? Have confidence in everything you serve, even if it wasn't what you were planning. Now, that's perfection.

"YOU MEAN *THIS* IS VEGAN?"

Vegan desserts are made without any animal products, so they are completely free of dairy and eggs. It may sound restrictive to cut out milk, cream, butter, and eggs from your ingredient list but, using a few simple substitutions, you won't taste the difference. Vegan desserts are perfect for children with allergies or anyone looking to eliminate cholesterol and saturated animal fat from their diet. Vegan baking is also a great way to practice kindness to animals, the planet, and yourself. If you want to satisfy your sweet tooth without busting your belt, look no further than my vegan Chocolate Mousse (page 199) or Salted Caramel Cupcakes (page 153). Vegan desserts are naturally lighter and less fattening than traditional baked goods, so you can have your cake and eat it, too!

READY, SET, BAKE

Bakers, start your ovens! Let's make some sweets. All of my recipes have been taste-tested and approved by vegans and butter lovers alike, so bake for anyone and everyone you know. Try this: Bake a batch of cupcakes for a co-worker, neighbor, or yoga teacher for no reason at all and watch how it brightens their day. I guarantee it will boost their mood and yours, too! Have fun and be sure to visit my online community at ChefChloe.com to let me know how everything tastes. Wishing you sweet success!

Live, Dream & Eat Dessert,

Chloe

Sweet Pantry

It doesn't matter how big or small your kitchen is, if you set up your pantry with these simple vegan essentials, you can bake just about anything. I always like to keep a stocked pantry, so that I can whip up something sweet the minute a craving hits!

FATS AND OILS

Canola Oil

Canola oil is my go-to baking oil. It is low in saturated fat, yet high in healthful omega-3 fatty acids. It is very mild tasting and has a high smoke point. All these qualities make it an excellent choice for baking and frying at high temperatures. Other mild tasting oils include vegetable, safflower, and grape-seed oil, all of which can be used in place of canola oil.

Coconut Oil

Coconut oil, which is pressed from *copra* (dried coconut meat) is one of the few saturated fats that does not come from an animal and is actually very healthful. It is high in lauric acid, which has many antiviral, antibacterial, and antioxidant properties that fight illnesses such as heart disease, diabetes, cancer, and HIV. It is also cholesterol and trans-fat free. It will keep on your pantry shelf for up to two years.

Coconut oil is solid at room temperature, which makes it great for baking. Unrefined coconut oil has a coconut flavor, while refined coconut oil does not. Feel free to substitute refined coconut oil for vegan margarine or vegetable shortening in equal proportions in my recipes. It works especially well as a substitute in frostings and pastry crusts.

Vegan Margarine

Vegan margarine is a terrific substitute for butter in vegan cooking and baking. My favorite brand of vegan margarine is Earth Balance, and it can be purchased in sticks or in a tub. It's made from a blend of oils and comes in soy-free varieties. It is all natural, non-hydrogenated, and trans-fat free. You can buy it at your local grocery store or natural foods market.

Non-hydrogenated Vegetable Shortening

Shortening is a solidified blend of oils that is great for making creamy frostings and flaky piecrusts. To make sure you are choosing the most healthful option, look for packaging that says "non-hydrogenated." Spectrum Organics and Earth Balance are excellent brands.

Olive Oil

Olive oil is rich in antioxidants and vitamin E, is a great source of heart-healthful monounsaturated fat, and helps to lower cholesterol. Olive oil lends a delicious rich flavor to baked goods, such as in my Lemon Olive-Oil Cake (page 135). If you prefer, you can use half olive oil and half canola oil in recipes calling for canola oil.

CHOCOLATE AND FLAVORINGS

Chocolate Chips

I use semisweet chocolate chips in many of my dessert recipes. They can be used whole or melted. Many brands, such as Ghirardelli or Guittard, make semisweet chocolate chips that are dairy free. You can also buy chocolate chips that are labeled "dairy free" or "vegan" at your local natural foods market.

Unsweetened Cocoa Powder

There are two types of unsweetened cocoa powder: Dutch-processed and natural. Dutch-processed cocoa powder goes through a process to soften the acidity of the cocoa, giving it a richer and less bitter flavor. I prefer to use Dutch-processed and recommend brands such as Valrhona or Droste. However, whichever kind of cocoa powder you have available will work just fine, as long as it is unsweetened.

Instant Espresso Powder

Espresso powder is a very dark and strong instant coffee. I use it in many of my dessert recipes for flavoring. I use Medaglia d'Oro brand, which can be found in the coffee aisle at any grocery store or purchased online. If you cannot find espresso powder, you can substitute the same amount of finely ground instant coffee. You may also use decaffeinated instant espresso or coffee.

Flavored Extracts

Adding a teaspoon or two of flavored extract is a great way to intensify flavor. When purchasing extracts, look for the word "pure" such as "pure vanilla extract" or "pure lemon extract" to avoid artificial flavors and chemicals.

Shredded Coconut

Shredded coconut, also known as *chopped coconut* or *coconut flakes,* adds extra flavor and texture to coconut cakes and pies. Feel free to use sweetened or unsweetened coconut. Toasting shredded coconut adds a little extra crunch to your dessert (see page 244).

Carob Chips

Carob, a legume, comes from the pods of the carob tree. Carob chips are a natural alternative to chocolate chips. I use carob chips in my PUPcakes (page 183) because carob is a dog-safe alternative to chocolate, which can be toxic to dogs. You can buy carob chips at your local natural foods market or online. Check to make sure that they are vegan because some brands contain dairy.

FLOURS

Wheat Flour

There are a variety of flours to cook and bake with. Many of my recipes call for unbleached all-purpose flour. This is also known as regular white flour, and it yields a light and tender product. Whole-wheat pastry flour is an unrefined alternative to all-purpose flour. If you prefer, you can use half whole-wheat pastry flour and half unbleached all-purpose flour.

Gluten-Free Flour

Bob's Red Mill Gluten-Free All-Purpose Baking Flour is an excellent product that can be substituted measure-for-measure in many of my recipes. It is made from a blend of garbanzo flour and potato starch, and can be found at your local grocery store or ordered online at BobsRedMill.com. There are many brands of gluten-free flour, but I find that I get the best results with Bob's Red Mill. When substituting gluten-free flour in a recipe, make sure that the other ingredients you are using in the recipe are labeled "gluten free" as well, such as chocolate chips, extracts, baking powder, and so on.

Note that while gluten-free flour can be used in almost all my dessert recipes with excellent results, it is very important to add xanthan gum (page 6) as directed in the recipe. Also, baking time may vary when using gluten-free flour.

Bread Flour

Bread flour is made from wheat and has a higher gluten and protein content than most flours. It works well in yeasted baked goods, and I use it in my recipe for New Orleans Beignets (page 27). It helps the pastry rise and gives it a nice doughy bite.

NONDAIRY MILK

There are many varieties of nondairy milk including soy, almond, rice, and coconut. They are healthful low-fat alternatives for anyone who wants to avoid dairy. Nondairy milk is often enriched with vitamins, and is free of cholesterol and lactose. It comes in plain, unsweetened, chocolate, and vanilla. You can purchase nondairy milk in refrigerated cartons or aseptic containers, which do not have to be refrigerated until opened and are perfect for lunch boxes and traveling.

Soy Milk

Soy milk is made from soybeans and water and has almost as much protein as cow's milk but is cholesterol free and low in saturated fat.

Almond Milk

Almond milk is made from pulverized almonds and water. The almond flavor is very subtle. Almond milk is thick and has added vitamins, such as calcium and vitamin D. It has no saturated fat, is cholesterol free, and very low in calories.

Rice Milk

Rice milk is a great alternative for those who are allergic to nuts or soy. Milled rice is mixed with water, creating a thinner milk, and is enriched with vitamins. It is low in sodium, has no saturated fat, and no cholesterol.

Coconut Milk

Coconut milk is thick and creamy, making it a great nondairy milk to use in decadent desserts. The fat in coconut milk is a healthful, so-called good fat, does not contribute to heart disease, and is beneficial to the cardiovascular system. You can buy coconut milk canned or in cartons in the refrigerated section of your grocery store. I prefer to use canned coconut milk, which is slightly thicker. With the exception of my Coconut Whipped Cream recipe (page 234) and Chocolate Mousse recipe (pages 181 and 199), you can substitute "lite" canned coconut milk, which is lower in fat.

PASTRY DOUGH

Phyllo dough

Phyllo, also spelled *filo,* is a very thin pastry dough popular in Mediterranean and Middle Eastern cooking. Phyllo dough can be found at your local grocery store in the freezer section, near the piecrusts. See my tip for working with phyllo dough on page 81.

Store-bought Piecrust

Store-bought piecrust is a great shortcut to use when you don't have time to roll dough. You can find it in the frozen aisle of any grocery store. Check the ingredient label to make sure the piecrust is vegan and non-hydrogenated. Most frozen piecrusts come in packages of two, perfect for making a double-crust pie.

SWEETENERS

Sugar

When choosing granulated or powdered sugar to bake with, I look for words like "organic", "fair-trade", and "vegan" on the package because some refined sugars are processed using animal bone char. Wholesome Sweeteners, Florida Crystals, and Whole Foods are all good quality brands that make specifically vegan, unrefined sugars.

Agave

Agave nectar is a natural, unrefined liquid sweetener that is extracted from the leaves of the Mexican agave plant. Agave has a sweeter flavor than sugar, and a lower glycemic index, too. I prefer to use light agave because of its mild flavor and clear color, but you can also buy it in darker varieties.

Maple Syrup

Pure maple syrup is a natural, unrefined liquid sweetener that is good for more than just pouring over pancakes. Its distinct maple taste adds flavor to cookies, icing, and frosting.

THICKENERS

Cornstarch and Arrowroot

Cornstarch is a fine powder made from corn kernels. Arrowroot is a fine powder made from the rootstalks of the arrowroot plant, which is a tropical tuber. Both cornstarch and arrowroot are used to thicken puddings, pie fillings, and custards. Arrowroot is a great alternative to cornstarch; they can be used interchangeably.

Xanthan Gum

Xanthan gum is a fine powder used for thickening, stabilizing, and emulsifying. I use xanthan gum when making ice cream from scratch because it adds a thick and stretchy quality. Xanthan gum is also a key ingredient in gluten-free baking. Whenever you use Bob's Red Mill Gluten-Free All-Purpose Baking Flour, it is best to add xanthan gum as directed on the back of the flour package. You can buy xanthan gum from most natural foods markets, or online at BobsRedMill.com.

EGG SUBSTITUTES

Baking Powder

Baking powder is a leavening agent that releases carbon dioxide gas into the batter, which causes bubbles and makes baked goods rise. Look for "aluminum free" on the package. Baking powder does not last forever. To see if your baking powder is still fresh, place a teaspoon of baking powder into a few tablespoons of warm water. If it bubbles immediately, your baking powder works. If not, it is time to replace it.

Baking Soda

Baking soda, like baking powder, is a leavening agent that causes baked goods to rise. The difference, however, is that baking soda should be combined with an acid, such as vinegar or lemon juice, for the most effective reaction. Just a teaspoon of baking soda combined with a couple tablespoons of acidic liquid will bind your baked goods together and act as an egg replacement. To see if your baking soda is still fresh, place a teaspoon of baking soda into a few tablespoons of vinegar. If it bubbles immediately, your baking soda works. If not, it is time to replace it.

Vinegar

Vinegar is an acidic liquid used frequently in vegan baking to replace eggs. When vinegar is combined with baking soda, a reaction occurs that enables baked goods to bind together and rise. Vinegar is also used to add tanginess and brighten the flavor of fruit in desserts, such as in my Cranberry-Pear Pie filling (page 106). I most often use white or apple cider vinegar. Balsamic vinegar will work as well, but be mindful that it might lend a dark color to your finished product.

EQUIPMENT

Blender

A blender is an important tool for making milkshakes, ice cream bases, or creamy pie fillings. You can use any type of blender for the recipes in this book. My favorite blender is a Vitamix, which is a high-speed, heavy-duty, powerful machine, available in restaurant supply stores, warehouse stores, and online. A lower-speed blender will work as well, just be sure to stop periodically and scrape down the sides with a spatula while blending.

Food Processor

A food processor is the workhorse of the kitchen. The processor can help you take shortcuts in your recipes by chopping nuts, grating carrots for carrot cake, pulsing pastry crust and pie dough, grinding chocolate, and so on. I recommend getting at least an eleven-cup capacity food processor, although you can always work with a smaller one in batches.

Stand or Hand Mixer

Electric stand mixers are useful for kneading dough, mixing batters, and beating frostings. If you do not have the kitchen space for a stand mixer, a hand-held electric mixer will work, too. KitchenAid is my brand of choice for both appliances.

Parchment Paper

Parchment paper is coated with silicone to make it nonstick. It is available in both rolls and sheets. Use it on baking sheets to prevent baked goods from sticking to the pan. Parchment paper is preferred to wax paper, because wax paper is not always oven safe.

Silpat

Silpat is a fiberglass and silicone nonstick baking mat that never needs greasing and can be used over and over again. It is available in various sizes and is easy to clean. If preferred, it can be used in place of parchment paper for baking.

Ice Cream Maker

Ice cream makers come in a range of shapes, sizes, and prices. You do not need to buy an expensive industrial ice cream maker to make my ice cream desserts. I've worked with small, inexpensive ice cream makers in some of the finest restaurants in New York City, and they worked just as well.

Ice Cream and Cookie Scoops

Ice cream and cookie scoops are great for scooping dough and batter evenly onto baking sheets or into cupcake pans. This will give your baked goods a professional, uniform look. For scooping cookie dough, I generally prefer a 1- or 2-tablespoon scoop. For scooping cupcake batter, I prefer a 4-tablespoon scoop for regular-sized cupcakes and a 1-tablespoon scoop for mini cupcakes.

Pastry Bags

There are many options when shopping for pastry bags: nylon, canvas, cloth, or disposable plastic. Any material will work; they can be purchased at your local baking-supply store or online. I recommend using a 14- to 16-inch bag for basic piping.

Pastry Tips

For piping frosting onto cupcakes, I like to use either a large star tip or a large round tip. I suggest #826 to #829 for a large star tip and #800 to #809 for a large round tip. For filling cupcakes, I prefer a small round tip, such as #4 or #5, or a Bismarck tip for extra precision.

Offset Spatula

The best tool for frosting a cake or cupcake by hand is an offset spatula. It is much easier to maneuver than using a knife and creates an even, smooth surface. For cupcakes, use a mini offset spatula.

Crème Brûlée Torch

A torch is a handy tool that can be used to caramelize sugar on desserts like Classic Crème Brûlée (page 201) or Oatmeal Brûlée with Caramelized Bananas (page 44). You can purchase a torch at your local kitchen supply store or hardware store.

Baking Sheets and Cake Pans

Baking sheets and cake pans come in all different shapes and sizes, but these are the ones I recommend keeping on hand:

- Two or three large, rimmed baking sheets (Make sure the baking sheets fit into your oven)
- Two 12-cup cupcake pans
- Two 24-cup mini cupcake pans, optional
- Two 9-inch round cake pans
- 9- x 13-inch pan
- 8-inch square pan
- Loaf or Bundt pan

Allergy-Free Baking

GLUTEN-FREE BAKING

Vegan and gluten-free baking go hand-in-hand. Most of the recipes in this book can easily be made gluten free.*

Flour is the main ingredient that needs to be replaced to make recipes gluten-free. Bob's Red Mill Gluten-Free All-Purpose Baking Flour is an excellent product that can be substituted measure-for-measure in many of my recipes. It is made from a blend of garbanzo flour and potato starch, and can be found at your local grocery store or ordered online at BobsRedMill.com. When substituting gluten-free flour in a recipe, make sure that the other ingredients you are using in the recipe are labeled "gluten free" as well, such as chocolate chips, extracts, baking powder, and so on.

Note that while gluten-free flour can be used in almost all of my dessert recipes with excellent results, it is very important to add xanthan gum (page 6) as directed in the recipe. Also, baking time may vary when using gluten-free flour.

SOY-FREE BAKING

Baking without soy is very easy in my book because my recipes do not rely on any soy-based ingredients like tofu, soy lecithin, or vegan cream cheese. When a recipe calls for nondairy milk, simply choose almond or rice milk instead of soy milk, and make sure you buy the soy-free variety of Earth Balance vegan margarine. Other ingredients, such as chocolate chips, may contain soy as well, so make sure each ingredient you purchase is specifically labeled "soy free."

SUGAR-FREE BAKING

Unrefined sweeteners, such as agave nectar or pure maple syrup, can be used in place of sugar in many of my recipes. The conversion is ⅔ cup liquid sweetener for every 1 cup sugar. If substituting a liquid sweetener, cut back on the liquid in the recipe (such as

---

* If you are preparing a recipe for yourself or someone else with a serious food allergy, check all ingredient labels carefully to make sure that they are allergen free. It is up to the consumer to avoid ingredients that contain allergens, allergen derivatives, or have been exposed to cross-contamination.

nondairy milk or water) by about ¼ cup. In addition, decrease the oven temperature by 25 degrees and increase the baking time slightly. To make cakes and cupcakes without refined sugar, use my recipes for Agave-Sweetened Vanilla Cake (page 187) and Agave-Sweetened Chocolate Cake (page 186) as your base. In addition, use Crème Anglaise (page 236) and fresh berries as a sugar-free topping for any dessert.

Dessert
for
Breakfast

New York–Style Crumb Cake

This is the ultimate New York–style breakfast cake—buttery and moist with a cinnamon-sugar crumble. Every New Yorker would agree that a slice of this is essential with your morning cup of joe!

Make-Ahead Tip:
Cake batter and crumb topping can be assembled in the pan, covered with plastic wrap, and refrigerated overnight. Bake fresh the next morning.

CRUMB TOPPING

1¼ cups all-purpose flour*	2 teaspoons ground cinnamon
⅓ cup sugar	¼ teaspoon salt
⅓ cup brown sugar	½ cup vegan margarine, melted

CAKE

1¼ cups all-purpose flour*	½ cup soy, almond, or rice milk
½ cup sugar	½ cup canola oil
1 teaspoon baking soda	1 teaspoon white or apple-cider
½ teaspoon baking powder	vinegar
¼ teaspoon salt	1 teaspoon pure vanilla extract

Powdered sugar, for serving

To make the crumb topping: In a medium bowl, combine flour, sugar, brown sugar, cinnamon, and salt. Add melted margarine and toss with 2 forks, as if you were tossing salad, until it appears crumbly. The crumbs should be the size of small peas.

To make the cake: Preheat the oven to 325 degrees. Lightly grease an 8-inch-square pan.

In a large bowl, whisk together flour, sugar, baking soda, baking powder, and salt. In a separate bowl, whisk together nondairy milk, oil, vinegar, and vanilla. Pour the wet mixture into the dry mixture and whisk until just combined. Do not overmix.

*For a gluten-free cake, substitute gluten-free all-purpose flour plus ½ teaspoon xanthan gum and see page 11. For a gluten-free crumb topping, substitute gluten-free all-purpose flour.

Fill the prepared pan with batter and evenly sprinkle with the crumb topping. Bake for about 40 minutes, or until a toothpick inserted in the center comes out dry with a few crumbs clinging to it. Let cool and dust with powdered sugar.

Raspberry Swirl Coffee Cake

MAKES ONE 8-INCH CAKE

This moist morning coffee cake is a must when preparing breakfast for guests. The beautiful swirls of raspberry add a nice tart flavor that balances the sweet pecan streusel. Your guests will be amazed by the flavor and even more amazed when you tell them that it's vegan!

Make-Ahead Tip:

Cake batter and streusel topping can be assembled in the pan, covered with plastic wrap, and refrigerated overnight. Bake fresh the next morning.

STREUSEL TOPPING

¼ cup all-purpose flour*	1 tablespoon ground cinnamon
1 cup roughly chopped pecans	½ teaspoon ground nutmeg
½ cup brown sugar	3 tablespoons canola oil

CAKE

2 cups all-purpose flour*	1 cup soy, almond, or rice milk
½ cup sugar	½ cup canola oil
¼ cup brown sugar	1 tablespoon white or apple cider
1 teaspoon baking soda	vinegar
1 teaspoon baking powder	2 teaspoons pure vanilla extract
½ teaspoon salt	2 cups raspberries, fresh or frozen

To make the streusel topping: In a medium bowl, combine flour, pecans, brown sugar, cinnamon, and nutmeg. Add oil and toss with 2 forks, as though you were tossing salad, until it appears crumbly. The crumbs should be the size of small peas.

To make the cake: Preheat the oven to 350 degrees. Lightly grease an 8-inch-square pan.

In a large bowl, whisk together flour, sugar, brown sugar, baking soda, baking powder, and salt. In a separate bowl, whisk together nondairy milk, oil, vinegar, and vanilla. Pour the

---

*For a gluten-free cake, substitute gluten-free all-purpose flour plus 1 teaspoon xanthan gum and see page 11. For a gluten-free streusel topping, substitute gluten-free all-purpose flour.

wet mixture into the dry mixture and whisk until just combined. Do not overmix. Gently fold in the raspberries.

Fill the prepared pan with batter and evenly sprinkle with the streusel topping. Bake for 40 minutes uncovered, then cover with foil, and bake for another 10 minutes. A toothpick inserted in the center of the cake should come out dry with a few crumbs clinging to it. Let cool and slice.

Chocolate Babka

If you've never tried chocolate babka (pronounced BOB-kuh), imagine a cross between a chocolate croissant and brioche. It's a luscious loaf of plush yeasted bread twisted with ribbons of fudgy chocolate. Cut and serve it like a cake at breakfast, lunch, or dinner. Beware: It's highly addictive. The addition of streusel adds another element of flavor and texture, but for a shortcut you can leave it out.

Make-Ahead Tip:

After the assembled unbaked babka has risen, it can be covered in plastic wrap in the pan and refrigerated overnight. Remove plastic wrap and bake the next day, following recipe directions.

FILLING

⅔ cup brown sugar

¼ cup all-purpose flour

2 tablespoons unsweetened cocoa
    powder

2 teaspoons ground cinnamon

4 tablespoons vegan margarine,
    room temperature

⅛ teaspoon salt

STREUSEL TOPPING

¼ cup sugar

3 tablespoons all-purpose flour

½ teaspoon ground cinnamon

¼ teaspoon salt

2 tablespoons vegan margarine,
    room temperature

DOUGH

2 cups all-purpose flour, plus extra for
    rolling

¼ cup sugar

1 packet active dry yeast (2¼ teaspoons)

½ teaspoon salt

¾ cup soy, almond, or rice milk,
    plus extra for brushing

½ cup vegan margarine

2 teaspoons pure vanilla extract

Canola oil, for greasing

Powdered Sugar, for serving

To make the filling: In a medium bowl, mix all ingredients and set aside.

To make the streusel topping: In a medium bowl, combine sugar, flour, cinnamon, and salt. Add margarine and toss with 2 forks, as though you were tossing salad, until it appears crumbly. The crumbs should be the size of small peas.

To make the dough: In the bowl of a stand mixer fitted with a whisk or paddle attachment, combine flour, sugar, yeast, and salt. In a medium saucepan, combine nondairy milk and margarine and heat to 110 degrees. Remove from heat and stir in vanilla. Gradually add the milk mixture to the flour mixture, while mixing on low speed. Once combined, increase speed to medium and beat for 10 to 12 minutes. The dough will be somewhat wet and sticky. Place the dough on a lightly floured surface and knead for about a minute or 2 with your hands. If needed, add a little bit of flour to keep the dough from sticking to your hands.

Transfer the dough to a large well-oiled bowl and rotate the ball of dough so it is completely covered with oil. This will prevent the dough from sticking to the bowl as it rises. Cover with a dry kitchen towel and place in a warm part of the kitchen. Let it sit until it has doubled in size, about 1½ hours (see Tip, page 23).

To assemble and bake the babka: Lightly grease an 8½- x 4-inch loaf pan and line with parchment paper long enough to overhang the 2 long edges.

On a lightly floured surface, roll the dough out into approximately a 20- x 12-inch rectangle. Crumble the filling over the dough, leaving a ½-inch border. With the short end towards you, roll the dough up evenly as though you are rolling a sleeping bag or yoga mat. Brush the top of the dough roll with nondairy milk and sprinkle half the streusel on top. Pat the streusel with your fingertips so it adheres to the dough.

Fold the roll in half, then lift and twist it once or twice (as though you are wringing a towel), and fit it into the prepared pan. Twisting the dough creates layers and allows the chocolate filling to disperse throughout the babka. Brush the top with more nondairy milk and sprinkle with remaining streusel. Cover with a dry kitchen towel and place in a warm part of the kitchen (see Tip, page 23) for the second rise until the babka has doubled in size, about 1½ hours.

Once the babka has risen, preheat the oven to 325 degrees. Bake, uncovered, for 40 to 45 minutes until the top is golden. Let the babka cool completely, then lift the parchment paper to unmold the babka. Dust with powdered sugar, slice, and serve. Leftover babka can be sliced and toasted the next day.

Chloe's Tip: Rising Dough

If your kitchen is cold, use this trick to create a warm environment for your dough to rise. Heat the oven to 200 degrees, then turn it off. Cover your bowl of dough with a dry kitchen towel, and place it in the oven to rise.

Tiramisu Pancakes

SERVES 2 TO 3

Tiramisu pancakes are perfect to make for dessert or a decadent breakfast. They are the most impressive pancakes on the planet: fluffy golden pancakes with a hint of espresso and rum, dotted with melted chocolate chips, and topped with a dollop of cool Coconut Whipped Cream (page 234).

1 cup all-purpose flour
1 tablespoon baking powder
1 tablespoon instant espresso powder
½ teaspoon salt
¾ cup water
¼ cup pure maple syrup

1 tablespoon dark rum
⅓ cup semisweet chocolate chips
　(dairy-free)
Canola oil, for greasing
Powdered sugar, for serving
Coconut Whipped Cream (page 234)

In a large bowl, whisk together flour, baking powder, espresso powder, and salt. In a separate small bowl, whisk together water, maple syrup, and dark rum. Add the liquid to the flour mixture and whisk until just combined. Do not overmix; the batter should have some lumps. Gently fold in chocolate chips.

Lightly oil a large nonstick skillet or griddle and heat over medium-high heat. Pour ¼ cup batter onto the skillet. When bubbles appear in the center of the pancake, it is time to flip it. Let it cook on the other side until lightly browned and cooked through, about 1 more minute. Repeat with remaining batter, adding more oil to the skillet as needed. If the batter becomes too thick, add a little more water, 1 tablespoon at a time. To serve, dust pancakes with powdered sugar and top with a dollop of Coconut Whipped Cream.

Sourdough French Toast

MAKES 14 SLICES

This recipe for French toast is so quick and easy. I love it with sourdough, but you can use whatever bread you have on hand. Any time I have overnight guests, they expect a batch of these in the morning. Luckily, the recipe is so simple that I always have the ingredients in my kitchen.

1 loaf sourdough or other bread, about 14 slices
2 cups all-purpose flour
2 cups soy, almond, or rice milk
3 tablespoons pure maple syrup, plus extra for serving

2 teaspoons pure vanilla extract
1 tablespoon ground cinnamon
¼ teaspoon salt
Canola oil, for greasing
Powdered sugar, for serving

Slice bread into ¾-inch thick slices. In a medium bowl, whisk together flour, nondairy milk, maple syrup, vanilla, cinnamon, and salt.

Submerge each slice of bread in the batter to coat. Meanwhile, lightly oil a large nonstick skillet or griddle and heat over medium-high heat. In batches, add coated bread to the skillet and let cook on each side until lightly browned and crisp. Repeat with remaining bread slices.

Dust with powdered sugar and serve with maple syrup.

New Orleans Beignets

MAKES ABOUT 70 BEIGNETS

That's right, a beignet (pronounced ben-YAY) can be made vegan! Beignets melt in your mouth when eaten fresh and warm with a light dusting of powdered sugar. I know this because I usually eat them standing over the stove. If you want to be fancy, plate them with a side of Chocolate Sauce (page 232) or Raspberry Sauce (page 233).

Make-Ahead Tip:

Dough can be stored in the refrigerator for up to 5 days. Undusted beignets can be kept warm in a 200 degree oven for up to 45 minutes before serving.

¼ cup vegan margarine

1 cup soy, almond, or rice milk

1½ cups water

½ cup sugar

1 packet active dry yeast (2¼ teaspoons)

6 cups bread flour, plus extra for rolling

1¼ teaspoons salt

Canola oil, for frying

Powdered sugar, for serving

Chocolate Sauce (page 232), optional

Raspberry Sauce (page 233), optional

In a medium saucepan melt margarine over medium heat. Stir in nondairy milk, water, and sugar until it reaches 110 degrees. Remove from heat, add yeast, and let sit for 5 minutes.

Meanwhile, in the bowl of a stand mixer fitted with a whisk or paddle attachment, combine flour and salt. Add yeast mixture and beat on low until incorporated. Beat for 1 more minute until the dough is wet and very sticky. Place the dough on a lightly floured surface and knead for about 2 minutes with your hands. If needed, add more flour to keep the dough from sticking to your hands.

Transfer the dough to a large well-oiled bowl and rotate the ball of dough, so that it is completely covered with oil. This will prevent the dough from sticking to the bowl as it rises. Cover the bowl with plastic wrap and chill in the refrigerator for 3 hours or overnight.

Remove from the refrigerator and punch down the dough. On a lightly floured surface, roll out the dough until it is about ¼ -inch thick. With a pizza cutter or sharp knife, cut the dough into approximately 2-inch squares.

Fill a deep-sided heavy skillet or deep fryer with about 2 inches of oil. Heat to 350 degrees, or until a small piece of dough sizzles when added to the oil. Fry the beignets in batches in the hot oil. Oil should sizzle around the beignets. Let each beignet fry for about 2 minutes, flip, and fry for about 1 minute more until golden brown. Drain on paper towels. Dust generously with powdered sugar and serve immediately. If desired, serve with Chocolate or Raspberry Sauce for dipping.

Apple Cider Doughnut Holes

MAKES ABOUT 43 DOUGHNUT HOLES

When I was in culinary school in New York City, I walked through the holiday bazaar at Columbus Circle one day and spotted a vendor selling apple cider doughnuts. I was bummed that they weren't vegan, so I went back to my apartment and, after several tries, came up with this delicious version. Serve these at your next holiday party or just get cozy and make a batch for yourself!

Note: The batter will need to chill in the refrigerator for 3 hours or overnight before frying.

COATING

1 cup sugar	1 teaspoon ground cinnamon

DOUGHNUTS

2⅔ cups all-purpose flour	1 cup apple cider or juice
⅔ cup sugar	¼ cup canola oil
2 teaspoons baking soda	¼ cup white or apple-cider vinegar
1 teaspoon ground nutmeg	1 teaspoon pure vanilla extract
1 teaspoon ground cinnamon	Canola oil, for frying
1 teaspoon salt	

To make the coating: In a small bowl, combine sugar and cinnamon. Set aside.

To make the doughnuts: In a large bowl, whisk together flour, sugar, baking soda, nutmeg, cinnamon, and salt. In a medium bowl, whisk together apple cider, oil, vinegar, and vanilla. Add the wet ingredients to the dry and stir together quickly until just combined. Do not overmix.

Refrigerate the batter, covered, for 3 hours or overnight. Once the batter is chilled, fill a deep-sided heavy skillet or deep fryer with about 2 inches of oil. Heat to 350 degrees, or until a small spoonful of batter sizzles when added to the oil. Using a cookie scoop, scoop about 1½ tablespoons of batter into the hot oil. Do not overcrowd the skillet; fry in batches. Let each doughnut fry for about 4 minutes, flipping occasionally, until crispy and lightly browned on all sides. Test for doneness by cutting into one doughnut to make sure it is cooked through. Adjust frying time accordingly. If doughnuts begin to lose their shape when frying, refrigerate the batter for about 10 minutes. Drain on paper towels and roll in cinnamon sugar. Serve immediately.

Baked Chocolate Doughnuts

MAKES 14 DOUGHNUTS

When I enter a doughnut shop, my eye always goes to the dark side of the bakery display case—the chocolate section, that is! But there's no need for fried, store-bought doughnuts when you can get the same chocolaty flavor from my homemade, baked chocolate doughnuts. Top them as you wish and enjoy your chocolate-on-chocolate creations.

DOUGHNUTS

2½ cups all-purpose flour

1 cup sugar

3 tablespoons unsweetened cocoa powder

2 teaspoons instant espresso powder

2 teaspoons baking soda

1 teaspoon salt

1¼ cup soy, almond, or rice milk

¼ cup canola oil

¼ cup white or apple-cider vinegar

1 teaspoon pure vanilla extract

CHOCOLATE GLAZE

¼ cup semisweet chocolate chips (dairy-free)

2 tablespoons plus 1 teaspoon soy, almond, or rice milk

½ cup powdered sugar

Optional toppings: Chocolate sprinkles, chopped toasted almonds, shredded coconut, and/or mini chocolate chips

To make the doughnuts: Preheat the oven to 375 degrees. Lightly grease two doughnut pans.

In a large bowl, whisk flour, sugar, cocoa, espresso powder, baking soda, and salt. In a separate bowl, whisk nondairy milk, oil, vinegar, and vanilla. Pour the wet mixture into the dry mixture and whisk until just combined. Do not overmix. The batter will be sticky.

Using a pastry bag or plastic bag with the tip cut, pipe the batter into the prepared doughnut pans and bake for 10 to 12 minutes. Remove the pans from the oven and let sit 5 minutes before unmolding.

To make the glaze: In a double boiler or microwave, melt chocolate chips and nondairy milk together. Whisk in powdered sugar until smooth. Let sit for 5 to 10 minutes, so that the glaze thickens and any powdered sugar clumps dissolve.

To assemble the doughnuts: Dip each doughnut into the glaze, coating the top. Twist the doughnut as you remove it from the glaze to give it a nice finish and prevent dripping. Immediately sprinkle the topping onto the glaze and let set.

Chloe's Vegan Desserts

Lemon Poppy Seed Muffins

MAKES 14 MUFFINS

Nothing says "Good morning, Sunshine!" like Lemon Poppy Seed Muffins and this recipe says it best. Light and zesty with a poppy seed crunch, these lemon iced muffins are worth waking up for!

Make-Ahead Tip:
Muffins can be made in advance and frozen for up to 1 month. Thaw and apply icing before serving.

MUFFINS

2 cups all-purpose flour*	½ cup canola oil
¾ cup sugar	¼ cup lemon juice
1 teaspoon baking powder	2 tablespoons lemon zest (about
½ teaspoon baking soda	2 lemons)
½ teaspoon salt	1 tablespoon pure lemon extract
1 cup coconut milk	1 tablespoon poppy seeds

ICING

1 cup powdered sugar	1 tablespoon water
3 to 4 teaspoons lemon juice	1 teaspoon lemon zest

To make the muffins: Preheat the oven to 400 degrees. Line a 12-cup cupcake pan with cupcake liners.

In a large bowl, whisk together flour, sugar, baking powder, baking soda, and salt. In a separate bowl, whisk together coconut milk, oil, lemon juice, zest, and lemon extract. Pour the wet mixture into the dry mixture and whisk until just combined. Fold in poppy seeds. Do not overmix.

Fill the cupcake liners about two-thirds full with batter. Bake for 15 minutes, or until a toothpick inserted in the center of the muffin comes out dry with a few crumbs clinging to it. Cool the muffins completely before icing.

*For a gluten-free alternative, substitute gluten-free all-purpose flour plus 1 teaspoon xanthan gum and see page 11.

To make the icing: Whisk the powdered sugar, lemon juice, water, and zest in a small bowl until smooth.

Spread a thin layer of icing over each muffin.

Pumpkin Cinnamon Rolls with Maple Glaze

MAKES 12 CINNAMON ROLLS

Holy pumpkin cinnamon rolly! I squeal with excitement every time I eat these and sometimes jump up and down when they come out of the oven. This is my mom's famous recipe, and it is nothing short of genius. The dough is so tender, moist, and fluffy that it puts every other cinnamon roll to shame. Everyone we serve these to says they are the best cinnamon rolls they have ever eaten. Now, you can be the judge!

Make-Ahead Tip:

After the assembled unbaked cinnamon rolls have risen, cover them in plastic wrap in the pan and refrigerate overnight. Remove plastic wrap and bake the next day, according to recipe directions.

DOUGH

1 cup pumpkin puree, canned or cooked fresh

1 cup soy, almond, or rice milk

½ cup plus 1 tablespoon sugar, divided

½ cup vegan margarine

½ teaspoon salt

1 teaspoon pure vanilla extract

¼ cup warm water, about 110 degrees

1 packet active dry yeast (2¼ teaspoons)

5 cups all-purpose flour, divided, plus extra for rolling

Canola oil, for greasing

FILLING

¾ cup brown sugar

2 tablespoons sugar

2 teaspoons ground cinnamon

4 tablespoons vegan margarine, melted

1 cup raisins

GLAZE

1½ cups powdered sugar

3 tablespoons maple syrup

1 to 3 tablespoons water

To make the dough: In a medium saucepan, whisk pumpkin puree, nondairy milk, ½ cup sugar, margarine, and salt over low heat until combined. Remove from heat and add vanilla. Let it cool until very warm to the touch, about 110 degrees.

While the pumpkin mixture is cooling, place the warm water, remaining 1 tablespoon sugar, and yeast in a 1-cup glass measuring cup. Stir for a second or two and set aside for about 10 minutes. The yeast will become foamy, double in size, and reach the ¾-cup line. If it does not do so, then the yeast is dead or the water was not at the proper temperature, so make another yeast mixture before proceeding to the next step.

In a stand mixer fitted with a whisk or paddle attachment, combine the pumpkin mixture and the yeast mixture, and beat at medium speed for about 1 minute. Reduce the speed to low, and add 2½ cups flour. Beat until incorporated and add the remaining 2½ cups flour. Beat for 1 more minute. The dough will be somewhat wet and sticky. Change to a dough hook attachment and knead on medium speed for 2 minutes.

Transfer the dough to a large well-oiled bowl and rotate the ball of dough, so that it is completely covered with oil. This will prevent the dough from sticking to the bowl as it rises. Cover with a dry kitchen towel and place in a warm part of the kitchen. Let it sit until it has doubled in size, about 1½ hours (see Tip, page 23).

Remove the kitchen towel and punch your fist in the center of the dough, so that the dough deflates. Take the dough out and put it on a floured surface, cover with the kitchen towel, and let rest for about 10 minutes.

To make the filling and assemble the rolls: Lightly grease a 9- x 13-inch pan. Combine brown sugar, sugar, and cinnamon in a small bowl and set aside.

Roll the dough out on a lightly floured surface into approximately a 20- x 13-inch rectangle.

Brush or spread the melted margarine over the entire surface of the dough. Sprinkle the sugar mixture and raisins evenly over the surface of the dough.

With the long end toward you, roll the dough up evenly. With the seam side down, use a sharp knife to cut the log in half. Then cut each half into 6 equal pieces. You will have 12 cinnamon rolls. Place the rolls, cut side up, into the prepared pan, in 4 rows with 3 rolls in each row, leaving some space between them. Cover with a dry kitchen towel and place in a warm part of the kitchen (see Tip, page 23) for the second rise until the cinnamon rolls have risen and expanded, about 1 hour.

Once the cinnamon rolls have risen, preheat the oven to 375 degrees. Bake, uncovered, for 20 to 25 minutes, until lightly browned on top. You can poke inside the rolls with a toothpick to make sure they are fully cooked through before removing from oven. Let the rolls cool for about 10 minutes before glazing.

To make the glaze: In a medium bowl, whisk together powdered sugar, maple syrup, and 1 tablespoon water at a time, until smooth.

Drizzle the glaze over the rolls. Serve warm or at room temperature.

Homemade Granola

This naturally sweetened gourmet granola can be eaten by the handful or sprinkled on nondairy yogurt, smoothies, or ice cream. It's my favorite gift to bring to dinner-party hosts because they can enjoy it for breakfast the next morning.

Make-Ahead Tip:
Can be made in advance and kept frozen for up to two months.

3 cups rolled oats	½ cup maple syrup or agave
¾ cup sliced almonds	2 tablespoons canola oil
2 teaspoons ground cinnamon	1 teaspoon pure vanilla extract
¼ teaspoon salt	1 cup raisins

Preheat the oven to 325 degrees. Line a large baking sheet with parchment paper or Silpat.

In a large bowl, combine oats, almonds, cinnamon, and salt, and mix with a large spoon. Add maple syrup, oil, and vanilla, and stir until oats are evenly coated. Spread the mixture onto the prepared baking sheet and bake for 30 to 40 minutes, turning occasionally with a spatula. Remove from oven, let cool completely, and mix in raisins.

Oatmeal Brûlée with Caramelized Bananas

Turning plain ole oatmeal into Oatmeal Brûlée is the brunch world's best-kept secret. By adding a simple sugar-torched top to oatmeal, your oats go from baby food to five-star hotel brunch. Top it with caramelized bananas for an extra-sweet touch, or keep it simple with fresh berries.

Make-Ahead Tip:

Oatmeal can be made in advance and refrigerated for up to 5 days or frozen in portions for up to 2 months. Reheat on the stovetop or in the microwave before torching.

OATMEAL

4 cups water

1 cup steel-cut oats

1 teaspoon pure vanilla extract

¼ teaspoon ground cinnamon

Sugar, for sprinkling

CARAMELIZED BANANAS

2 large ripe bananas

¼ cup sugar

2 teaspoons canola oil,
    plus more as needed

To make the oatmeal: In a medium saucepan, bring water to a boil. Add oats and reduce heat to simmer. Keep at a low simmer, uncovered, for 25 to 30 minutes, or until oats are tender and water is mostly absorbed. Stir occasionally. Remove from heat, and stir in vanilla and cinnamon. Distribute the oatmeal evenly into ramekins, bowls, or coffee mugs.

Sprinkle about 2 teaspoons sugar onto each ramekin. For each ramekin, hold your torch about 2 to 3 inches from the sugar and melt the sugar until it bubbles and turns slightly golden. Be sure to move your torch back and forth continuously, so that it does not burn in one spot. Continue to torch until there is no more visible dry sugar. Let sit for 3 to 5 minutes.

To make the caramelized bananas: Slice bananas into ½-inch slices on the diagonal. Roll the bananas in sugar until each piece is completely coated.

In a large nonstick skillet, heat oil over medium-high heat. In batches, add the sugar-coated bananas. Let cook 3 to 4 minutes, or until lightly browned and caramelized. Flip using a spatula or tongs, and let cook another minute or so. Once both sides are nicely caramelized, transfer to a parchment-lined baking sheet or plate, so that the bananas do not stick. Before beginning each batch, wipe pan with a paper or kitchen towel and add more oil as needed.

Top each serving of oatmeal with a few caramelized banana slices and serve immediately.

Cookies
and Bars

Lemon Bars

The only thing that excites a crowd more than chocolate is a platter of lemon bars! Lemon bars are my favorite dessert to serve after a heavy meal because the tangy lemon filling is light and refreshing. Sifting powdered sugar over the bars is a simple way to create an elegant, bakery-style presentation.

Note: The lemon bars will need to chill in the refrigerator for 8 hours or overnight before serving.

SHORTBREAD CRUST

½ cup vegan margarine	⅓ cup sugar
1½ cups all-purpose flour	¼ teaspoon salt

FILLING

1 cup soy, almond, or rice milk, divided	⅔ cup lemon juice
6 tablespoons cornstarch or arrowroot	2 tablespoons lemon zest (about 2 lemons)
¼ cup all-purpose flour	Natural yellow food coloring, optional
2 cups sugar	

Powdered sugar, for serving

To make the shortbread crust: Preheat the oven to 350 degrees. Lightly grease an 8-inch square pan and line with parchment paper long enough to overhang the edges. Lightly grease the parchment paper.

In a food processor, pulse margarine, flour, sugar, and salt until crumbly. Press into the prepared pan. Bake for 18 minutes. Remove from oven and let cool.

To make the filling: In a small bowl, whisk ½ cup nondairy milk, cornstarch, and flour until completely smooth. Set aside.

In a medium saucepan, combine remaining ½ cup nondairy milk, sugar, and lemon juice, and bring to a boil. Reduce heat to medium and slowly whisk in cornstarch mixture. Continue to cook, whisking continuously, for about 5 minutes until very thick, like pudding. Remove from heat and stir in lemon zest and food coloring, if using.

To make the lemon bars: Pour the filling over the crust and bake for 15 minutes. Let cool, then chill in the refrigerator for 8 hours or overnight. Once chilled and set, lift the parchment paper to release the bars from the pan and unmold. Using a sharp knife, cut into 2-inch squares and dust with powdered sugar.

Blondies

MAKES SIXTEEN 2-INCH SQUARES

It may be true that blondes have more fun, because these bars always start a party in my mouth! These brown sugary blondies are crispy around the edges and chewy in the center, with a hint of cinnamon and rum, which really boosts the flavor. Try making these for die-hard brownie fans and they may just go blond forever!

1 cup all-purpose flour	1 tablespoon pure vanilla extract
¾ teaspoon baking powder	1 tablespoon dark rum or bourbon,
½ teaspoon ground cinnamon	optional
¼ teaspoon salt	⅓ cup semisweet chocolate chips
6 tablespoons vegan margarine	(dairy-free)
¾ cup brown sugar	⅓ cup chopped walnuts

Preheat the oven to 350 degrees. Lightly grease an 8-inch square pan and line with parchment paper long enough to overhang the edges.

In a medium bowl, whisk flour, baking powder, cinnamon, and salt until combined. Set aside. Using a stand or hand mixer, beat the margarine, brown sugar, vanilla, and rum, if using, until combined. Slowly beat in the flour mixture. Once the flour mixture is incorporated, add chocolate chips and walnuts. The batter will be thick.

Evenly pat the batter into the prepared pan. Bake for 25 minutes, until lightly browned around the edges. Once cooled, lift the parchment paper to release the blondies from the pan and unmold. Using a sharp knife, cut into 2-inch squares and serve.

Brownies

Brownies made with a combination of cocoa powder and melted chocolate yield a richer chocolate flavor than those that call for only one chocolate source. Many vegan brownie recipes rely on ingredients such as applesauce or flaxseed to replace the eggs, but I find that the tastiest method is simply using the right proportion of baking powder. This easy recipe makes a fudgy brownie that is extremely moist with a thin crackly top, which is exactly how I like it.

¾ cup vegan margarine

1½ cups semisweet chocolate chips
   (dairy-free)

2 cups sugar

1½ cups all-purpose flour

½ cup unsweetened cocoa powder

1½ teaspoons baking powder

½ teaspoon salt

½ cup soy, almond, or rice milk

1 tablespoon pure vanilla extract

½ cup chopped walnuts, optional

Preheat the oven to 350 degrees. Lightly grease a 9- by 13-inch pan and line with parchment paper long enough to hang over the edges.

In a double boiler or microwave, heat margarine and chocolate chips until completely melted. Whisk until smooth and set aside.

In the bowl of a stand mixer, combine sugar, flour, cocoa, baking powder, and salt. Mix on low until combined. Add melted chocolate and margarine and continue to mix until a crumbly consistency forms. Add nondairy milk and vanilla extract and beat on medium-high for 30 seconds, stopping once to scrape down the sides of the bowl, until smooth.

Evenly spread the batter into the prepared pan and top with walnuts, if using. Bake for 45 minutes. The center of the brownie will be slightly wet and not fully set. Let the brownies cool completely, then lift the parchment paper to release the brownies from the pan and unmold. Using a sharp knife, remove the hard edges and cut the remaining brownie into small squares or oversized bars (see Tip, page 53). Store brownies in the refrigerator until serving.

Chloe's Tip: Cutting Bar Cookies

Here is a neat trick for cutting brownies and bar cookies into oversized perfect rectangles like the upscale bakeries do. Take one card from a deck of playing cards and use it as your template for each piece. For a 9- x 13-inch pan, you will get approximately 10 brownies.

Pecan Bars

My mom veganized her famous family recipe for pecan bars and, let me tell you, it is better than any pecan bar I've ever tasted—vegan or not! I ate half the batch the first time I tasted them, so consider yourself warned. Thank you, Mommy, for letting me share this unbelievably good recipe.

Note: The bar cookies will need to chill in the refrigerator for 8 hours or overnight before serving.

SHORTBREAD CRUST

½ cup vegan margarine	⅓ cup sugar
1½ cups all-purpose flour	¼ teaspoon salt

FILLING

⅓ cup brown sugar	2 tablespoons soy, almond, or rice
¼ cup sugar	milk
4 tablespoons vegan margarine	2 cup pecans, toasted and roughly
¼ cup agave	chopped
	1 teaspoon pure vanilla extract

To make the shortbread crust: Preheat the oven to 350 degrees. Line an 8-inch square pan with parchment paper long enough to overhang the edges.

In a food processor, pulse margarine, flour, sugar, and salt until crumbly. Press firmly into the prepared pan and bake for 25 minutes. Remove from oven and let cool.

To make the filling: In a medium saucepan, combine brown sugar, sugar, margarine, agave, and nondairy milk and bring to a boil. Reduce heat and let simmer, about 5 minutes. Remove from heat and stir in the pecans and vanilla. Spread the filling over the shortbread crust. Let cool completely and chill in the refrigerator for 8 hours or overnight until filling has set.

Once chilled and set, lift the parchment paper to release the bars from the pan and unmold. Using a sharp knife, cut into 2-inch squares.

Chocolate Peanut Butter Fudge

MAKES SIXTEEN 2-INCH SQUARES

These sweet and salty layers of peanut butter and decadent chocolate fudge will melt in your mouth with each bite. Keep in mind that these are super rich, so a little piece goes a long way.

Note: The fudge will need to chill in the refrigerator for 8 hours or overnight before serving.

PEANUT BUTTER LAYER

1 cup creamy peanut butter
1 cup vegan margarine

1 teaspoon pure vanilla extract
3 cups powdered sugar

CHOCOLATE LAYER

½ cup soy, almond, or rice milk
1½ cups semisweet chocolate chips
   (dairy-free)
1½ cups powdered sugar

2 tablespoons unsweetened cocoa
   powder
½ cup chopped roasted peanuts

Generously line an 8-inch square pan with foil, so that it covers all sides and hangs over the edges of the pan.

To make the peanut butter layer: In a medium saucepan, whisk peanut butter and margarine over low heat until the mixture is melted and smooth. Remove from heat and whisk in vanilla. Transfer to the bowl of a stand mixer and add powdered sugar. Beat until combined. Press the mixture into the prepared pan.

To make the chocolate layer: In a medium saucepan, cook and whisk nondairy milk and chocolate chips over low heat until chocolate is melted and smooth.

In the bowl of a stand mixer, combine powdered sugar and cocoa. Add the melted chocolate mixture and beat until all ingredients are incorporated and smooth. Evenly spread the chocolate layer over the peanut butter layer in the prepared pan. Top with peanuts and pat down lightly.

Cover tightly with foil and refrigerate for 8 hours or overnight. Bring to room temperature and cut into 2-inch squares to serve.

Beach Cookies

My favorite cookies growing up were my mom's famous beach cookies. Beach cookies are ooey-gooey bar cookies with layers of cookie crust, creamy coconut, chocolate chips, and chopped nuts. These cookies earned their name because my mom always packed them when she took my brother Andy and me to the beach. We always packed way too many, so I would walk around to sunbathers and offer them cookies!

Note: The cookies will need to chill in the refrigerator for 8 hours or overnight before serving.

½ cup vegan margarine, melted

2 cups vegan cookie or graham cracker crumbs*

1 cup canned coconut milk, mixed well before measuring

¼ cup agave or pure maple syrup

1 teaspoon pure vanilla extract

⅛ teaspoon salt

2 tablespoons cornstarch or arrowroot

1½ cups shredded coconut

2 cups semisweet chocolate chips (dairy-free)

½ cup chopped walnuts, toasted, optional

Preheat the oven to 350 degrees.

Pour margarine into a 9-x 13-inch baking pan. Tilt the pan to swirl the margarine around until the bottom of the pan is completely coated. Sprinkle crumbs evenly into the pan until the bottom of the pan is evenly coated in crumbs. Pat down lightly.

In a medium bowl, whisk together coconut milk, agave, vanilla, salt, and cornstarch. Drizzle this mixture evenly over the crumb layer. Sprinkle shredded coconut into the pan, then layer chocolate chips and walnuts. With the palm of your hand, gently pat so that the chocolate chips are firmly pressed into the cookie.

Bake for 25 to 30 minutes, or until center looks thick and slightly bubbly with lightly browned edges. Let cool, and then refrigerate for 8 hours or overnight. Using a sharp knife, cut into small squares.

*For a gluten-free alternative, substitute gluten-free cookies and see page 11.

Double-Crust Fudge Bars

MAKES SIXTEEN 2-INCH BARS

This is my favorite bar cookie of the chapter because there is no better topping than crust itself. Crust lovers, say goodbye to the stress of claiming an end piece! Each bar is abundant in buttery shortbread crust and rich, not-too-sweet chocolate fudge. Walnuts may be added for a little extra crunch and flavor.

Note: The cookies will need to chill in the refrigerator for 8 hours or overnight before serving.

SHORTBREAD CRUST

2 cups all-purpose flour	½ cup sugar
1 cup vegan margarine	½ teaspoon salt

FILLING

¾ cup canned coconut milk, mixed well before measuring	¼ cup sugar
2 cups semisweet chocolate chips (dairy-free)	½ cup chopped walnuts, optional

To make the shortbread crust: Preheat the oven to 350 degrees. Lightly grease an 8-inch square pan and line with parchment paper long enough to overhang the edges.

In a food processor, pulse flour, margarine, sugar, and salt until crumbly. Reserve 1 cup of dough for topping, and press the remaining dough into the prepared pan.

To make the filling: In a medium saucepan, combine coconut milk, chocolate chips, and sugar. Stir over low heat until chocolate is melted. Remove from heat and stir in nuts.

To make the bars: Pour the filling over the unbaked crust and crumble the reserved shortbread dough over the top, leaving some of the dough in larger clumps.

Bake for 35 minutes. Let cool, then chill in the refrigerator for 8 hours or overnight. Once chilled and set, lift the parchment paper to release the bars from the pan and unmold. Using a sharp knife, cut into 2-inch squares, and serve.

Chocolate Chip Cookies

MAKES ABOUT SIXTY 2½-INCH COOKIES

This is my vegan version of America's favorite cookie. With crisp golden edges, and soft, chewy centers, these chocolate chip cookies are nothing short of classic. I keep a batch of already-scooped dough in my freezer at all times in case I have unexpected guests or a sudden cookie craving.

Make-Ahead Tip:
Cookie dough can be made in advance and kept refrigerated for up to 1 week or frozen for up to 1 month.

2¼ cups all-purpose flour*
1 tablespoon cornstarch or arrowroot
1 teaspoon baking soda
¾ teaspoon salt
1 cup vegan margarine
¾ cup brown sugar

¾ cup sugar
¼ cup water
1 tablespoon pure vanilla extract
1½ cups semisweet chocolate chips
  (dairy-free)
1 cup chopped pecans, optional

Preheat the oven to 350 degrees. Line 2 or 3 large baking sheets with parchment paper or Silpat.

In a medium bowl, whisk together flour, cornstarch, baking soda, and salt. Set aside.

Using a stand or hand mixer, beat margarine, brown sugar, sugar, water, and vanilla until fluffy. Slowly beat in the flour mixture. Once the flour mixture is incorporated, add chocolate chips and pecans. Scoop about 1 rounded tablespoon of dough at a time onto the prepared baking sheets, leaving about 2 inches between each scoop. Bake for 10 to 12 minutes, or until the edges are golden. Let cool on the pan and serve.

*For a gluten-free alternative, substitute gluten-free all-purpose flour plus ½ teaspoon xanthan gum and see page 11.

Chloe's Tip: Cookies in a Jar

For a sweet birthday or holiday gift, layer up the dry ingredients from my Chocolate Chip Cookie recipe in a jar. Give it to someone with the recipe attached, or better yet, a copy of this book! Whenever they're craving hot, freshly baked chocolate chip cookies, they can whip 'em up and think of you.

Chloe O's

Sure, Oreos are technically vegan, but it's much more fun to make Chloe O's from scratch! Plus, this recipe is all natural and great for kids with allergies.

Make-Ahead Tip:
Cookie dough can be made in advance and kept refrigerated for up to 1 week or frozen for up to 1 month.

COOKIES

1¼ cups all-purpose flour*	½ cup vegan margarine
1 cup sugar	3 tablespoons soy, almond,
½ cup unsweetened cocoa powder	or rice milk
¼ teaspoon salt	1 teaspoon pure vanilla extract
¼ teaspoon baking soda	

FILLING

¼ cup non-hydrogenated vegetable shortening	2 cups powdered sugar
¼ cup vegan margarine	1 teaspoon pure vanilla extract

To make the cookies: In a food processor, pulse flour, sugar, cocoa, salt, and baking soda until combined. Add margarine, milk, and vanilla. Process until the mixture comes together and forms a dough. Chill the dough in the refrigerator, covered, for 1 hour.

Preheat the oven to 350 degrees. Line 2 large baking sheets with parchment paper or Silpat. Roll a heaping teaspoon of dough into a ball and place onto prepared baking sheets, leaving about 3 inches between each ball. Evenly flatten the dough with the palm of your hand so that it is about ¼ inch thick and bake for about 12 minutes. Let cool on the pan.

To make the filling: Using a handheld or stand mixer, beat shortening and margarine until smooth and fluffy. With the mixer running on low, add powdered sugar and vanilla, and

*For a gluten-free alternative, substitute gluten-free all-purpose flour plus ¼ teaspoon xanthan gum and see page 11.

beat until incorporated. Increase speed to high and beat for 2 more minutes until light and fluffy.

To assemble the cookies: Spread a layer of filling on the flat bottom side of a cookie. Place the flat bottom side of another cookie on top of the filling. Lightly press the cookies together. Repeat with remaining cookies.

Oatmeal Raisin Cookies

I like to bake these cookies on rainy days, in my pajamas, with my dogs at my feet waiting for me to drop an oat. Nothing says comfort cookie quite like the cinnamon aroma of warm oatmeal raisin cookies. Turn these into "everything" cookies by adding chocolate chips, shredded coconut, chopped nuts, and/or dried cranberries.

Make-Ahead Tip:

Cookie dough can be made in advance and kept refrigerated for up to 1 week or frozen for up to 1 month.

1¼ cups all-purpose flour*
1 teaspoon ground cinnamon
½ teaspoon ground nutmeg
½ teaspoon baking soda
½ teaspoon salt
¾ cup vegan margarine

1 cup brown sugar
¼ cup sugar
1 tablespoon pure vanilla extract
1 tablespoon water
2 cups rolled oats
1 cup raisins

Preheat the oven to 350 degrees. Line 2 or 3 large baking sheets with parchment paper or Silpat.

In a medium bowl, whisk together flour, cinnamon, nutmeg, baking soda, and salt. Set aside.

Using a stand or hand mixer, beat margarine, brown sugar, sugar, vanilla, and water until well combined. Slowly beat in the flour mixture. Once the flour mixture is incorporated, fold in oats and raisins. Scoop about 2 tablespoons of dough at a time onto the prepared baking sheets, leaving about 4 inches between each scoop. Bake for 12 to 14 minutes, or until the edges are golden. Let cool on the pan and serve.

*For a gluten-free alternative, substitute gluten-free all-purpose flour plus ¼ teaspoon xanthan gum and see page 11.

Vermont Maple Cookies

MAKES ABOUT SIXTEEN 3-INCH SANDWICH COOKIES

My friend Laura lives in Vermont, and she sent me the most delicious Vermont maple syrup for my twenty-third birthday. After one taste, I was tempted to drink the whole bottle, but instead, I let it inspire this recipe!

Make-Ahead Tip:
Cookie dough can be made in advance and kept refrigerated for up to 1 week or frozen for up to 1 month.

COOKIES

2½ cups all-purpose flour*	¾ cup vegan margarine
1 cup sugar	4 tablespoons pure maple syrup
½ teaspoon baking soda	2 tablespoons water

FILLING

½ cup vegan margarine	5 tablespoons pure maple syrup
2½ cups powdered sugar	

To make the cookies: Preheat oven to 350 degrees. Line 2 or 3 large baking sheets with parchment paper or Silpat.

In a food processor, combine flour, sugar, and baking soda. Add margarine, maple syrup, and water. Pulse until soft and doughy.

On a lightly floured surface, roll the dough out until it is ¼ inch thick, working with half the dough at a time. Using a 3-inch cookie cutter, cut out as many shapes as you can. You can combine any remaining scraps to roll and cut more cookies. If the dough gets too soft to work with, refrigerate it for 5 to 10 minutes.

Place the shapes on the prepared baking sheets about ½ inch apart. Bake for 10 to 12 minutes until lightly golden around the edges. Let cool on the pan.

*For a gluten-free alternative, substitute gluten-free all-purpose flour plus ½ teaspoon xanthan gum and see page 11.

To make the filling: Using a handheld or stand mixer, beat the margarine until smooth. With the mixer running on low, add powdered sugar and maple syrup. Increase the speed to high and beat for 2 more minutes until light and fluffy.

To assemble the cookies: Spread a layer of filling on the flat bottom side of a cookie. Place the flat bottom side of another cookie on top of the filling. Lightly press the 2 cookies together. Repeat with remaining cookies. Refrigerate the cookies to help set, if needed.

Peanut Butter Cookies

This is my simple recipe for classic peanut butter cookies. Using brown sugar yields a soft, chewy center. Add chocolate chips or chopped peanuts for extra crunch.

Make-Ahead Tip:

Cookie dough can be made in advance and kept refrigerated for up to 1 week or frozen for up to 1 month.

1¼ cups all-purpose flour*	½ cup vegan margarine
¾ teaspoon baking soda	1 cup brown sugar
½ teaspoon salt	2 teaspoons pure vanilla extract
¾ cup peanut butter, creamy or crunchy	1 tablespoon water

Preheat the oven to 350 degrees. Line 2 or 3 large baking sheets with parchment paper or Silpat.

In a medium bowl, whisk together flour, baking soda, and salt. Set aside.

Using a stand or hand mixer, beat peanut butter, margarine, brown sugar, vanilla, and water until fluffy. Slowly beat in the flour mixture. If the dough is too dry, add a little extra water, 1 tablespoon at a time. Scoop about 2 tablespoons of dough at a time onto the prepared baking sheets, leaving about 4 inches between each scoop. Score the dough using the back of a fork (see Tip). Bake for 12 to 14 minutes, or until the edges are lightly browned. Let cool on the pan and serve.

Chloe's Tip: How to Score a Peanut Butter Cookie

Peanut butter cookies can often be recognized by their bakery-style grid design, which adds extra crunch. To achieve this look, gently press the back of a fork on top of each scoop of cookie dough, rolling through the prongs. Repeat this motion once more, perpendicular to your first mark.

*For a gluten-free alternative, substitute gluten-free all-purpose flour plus ¼ teaspoon xanthan gum and see page 11.

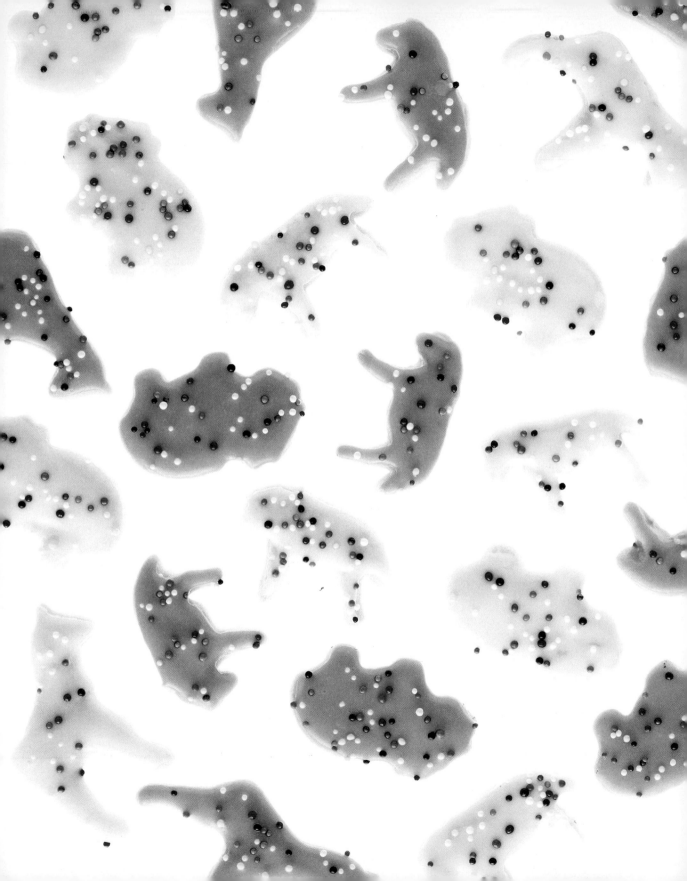

Animal Cookies

There is something so beautiful and nostalgic about animal cookies, from the delicate animal shapes to the tiny rainbow sprinkles. Skip the ones from the bag and try my homemade vegan version.

Make-Ahead Tip:
Cookie dough can be made in advance and kept refrigerated for up to 1 week or frozen for up to 1 month.

COOKIES

1¼ cups all-purpose flour*	½ cup vegan margarine
½ cup sugar	1 to 2 tablespoons water
¼ teaspoon baking soda	½ teaspoon pure vanilla extract
Cookie Icing (page 238)	Sprinkles

To make the cookies: Preheat oven to 350 degrees. Line 2 or 3 large baking sheets with Silpat or parchment paper.

In a food processor, combine flour, sugar, and baking soda. Add margarine, 1 tablespoon water, and vanilla. Pulse until soft and doughy. If needed, add 1 more tablespoon water.

Working with half the dough at a time, place the dough between two large sheets of floured parchment paper. Roll dough out until it is ¼ inch thick. Gently peel off the top sheet of parchment paper. Using a 1-inch cookie cutter, cut out as many shapes as you can. You can combine any remaining scraps to roll and cut more cookies.

Place the shapes on the prepared baking sheets about ½ inch apart. Bake for 8 to 10 minutes until lightly golden around the edges. Let cool on the pan.

To decorate the cookies: Place the cookies on a wire rack and, using a small offset spatula, generously ice them so that they are thoroughly coated, allowing any excess icing to drip off the sides. Immediately decorate with sprinkles. Let the icing on the cookies set, then serve.

*For a gluten-free alternative, substitute gluten-free all-purpose flour plus ¼ teaspoon xanthan gum and see page 11.

Black-and-White Cookies

There isn't a deli in NYC that doesn't display these beauties in the window. Black-and-White Cookies are a cake-cookie hybrid with a smooth, glossy glaze. Try my veganized version and see which side of the cookie you like best!

COOKIES

1¼ cups all-purpose flour

½ cup sugar

½ teaspoon baking powder

½ teaspoon baking soda

½ teaspoon salt

⅓ cup canola oil

⅓ cup soy, almond, or rice milk

1 tablespoon lemon juice

1 teaspoon pure vanilla extract

ICING

4 cups powdered sugar

6 tablespoons water, divided

2 tablespoons unsweetened cocoa powder

2 teaspoons lemon juice

To make the cookies: Preheat the oven to 350 degrees. Line 2 or 3 large baking sheets with parchment paper or Silpat.

In a large bowl, whisk together flour, sugar, baking powder, baking soda, and salt. In a separate bowl, whisk together oil, nondairy milk, lemon juice, and vanilla. Pour the wet mixture into the dry mixture and whisk until almost smooth. The batter will be thick.

Scoop about ¼ cup batter at a time onto the prepared baking sheets, leaving about 3 inches between each scoop. Gently flatten the dough with the palm of your hand and shape into a dome. Bake for 16 to 18 minutes, or until golden around the edges. Let cool on the pan.

To make the icing: In a medium bowl, whisk together powdered sugar and 5 tablespoons water until smooth. For the chocolate icing, transfer ¾ cup of the icing mixture to a separate small bowl and whisk in cocoa and remaining 1 tablespoon water. Add an extra teaspoon of water to the chocolate icing if it is too thick. Add lemon juice to the remainder of the white icing and whisk. If either icing gets too thick as it sits, add more water, a little at a time.

To assemble the cookies: Using a small offset spatula or knife, spread a thin layer of white icing over half of the bottom side of each cookie. Then spread a thin layer of chocolate icing over the other half of each cookie. Let set at room temperature and serve.

Lemon Thyme Tea Cookies

MAKES 25 SMALL SQUARES

Before these cookies even hit the oven, the scent of lemon and thyme wafts through the house and everyone comes down to see what's cooking. These delicate, buttery cookies are packed with flavor and simply perfect with an afternoon cup of tea. This is also a great treat to whip up the day after Thanksgiving when you have leftover thyme from your favorite stuffing recipe.

1¾ cup all-purpose flour
½ cup powdered sugar
¼ teaspoon salt
2 teaspoons chopped thyme leaves
    (see Tip)

4 tablespoons lemon zest
    (about 4 lemons)
¾ cup vegan margarine

Preheat the oven to 350 degrees. Lightly grease an 8-inch square pan and line with parchment paper long enough to overhang the edges.

In a food processor, pulse flour, sugar, salt, thyme, and zest until combined. Add margarine and pulse until crumbly and incorporated. Press the dough firmly into the prepared pan and pat the top until smooth. Bake for 20 minutes, until very lightly browned around the edges. Let cool in the pan.

Once cooled, lift the parchment paper to release the cookies from the pan and unmold. Using a sharp knife, cut into 25 squares.

Chloe's Tip: Removing Thyme Leaves

To remove thyme leaves from the stem, hold the stem with one hand and slide your thumb and index finger of the other hand along the stem, against the direction in which the leaves are growing. Let the thyme leaves fall off easily onto your cutting board.

Baklava

MAKES ABOUT 28 PIECES

Ooh-la-la baklava—sticky sweet pistachio filling with a flaky phyllo crust! This traditional Turkish dessert may seem fancy and difficult to make, but it is actually quite easy. It just looks fancy!

1 cup sugar

1 cup water

2 tablespoons agave

1 teaspoon pure vanilla extract

½ cup walnuts

½ cup shelled pistachios

½ cup brown sugar

1 teaspoon ground cinnamon

½ cup vegan margarine, melted

1 pound phyllo dough, thawed according to package directions (see Tip, page 81), and trimmed to fit in a 9- x 13-inch pan

Preheat the oven to 350 degrees.

In a medium saucepan, combine sugar, water, and agave. Bring to a boil and let cook on medium-high for 20 minutes. Remove from heat and stir in vanilla. Set aside and let cool.

In a food processor, combine walnuts, pistachios, brown sugar, and cinnamon. Pulse until coarsely chopped and set aside.

Lightly brush a 9- x 13-inch rimmed baking sheet with melted margarine. Lay 2 sheets of phyllo dough in the baking sheet. Brush with melted margarine, and layer 2 more sheets of phyllo. Repeat this process so that there are 6 sheets of phyllo in the baking sheet. Brush the top layer with melted margarine and sprinkle with about ½ cup of the nut mixture. Layer 2 more sheets of phyllo on top of the nut mixture and brush the top with melted margarine. Repeat this process, layering ½ cup of the nut mixture and 2 sheets phyllo, until you have used all of the nut mixture. The top phyllo layer should have about 6 to 8 sheets of phyllo, brushed with melted margarine between every 2.

Before baking, use a sharp knife or pizza cutter to slice diamond or square pieces. Bake for about 45 minutes until golden. Remove from oven and pour the sugar syrup evenly over the baked pastry. Let sit, uncovered, until completely cooled, and serve.

Chloe's Tip: Phyllo Dough

Phyllo dough can be found at your local grocery store, in the freezer section, near the piecrusts. Thaw frozen packages of phyllo dough according to package directions. After unwrapping a package of phyllo dough, immediately cover the phyllo sheets with a slightly damp towel so that they do not dry out. Don't sweat it if the phyllo sheets tear and wrinkle. Imperfections will not be noticeable on the finished product. This is part of making a rustic flaky pastry!

Mojito Chocolate Chip Cookies

MAKES ABOUT FORTY-SIX 2½-INCH COOKIES

This recipe mash-up combines the best elements of mojitos and chocolate chip cookies in one! The lime zest adds beautiful green flecks to an otherwise seemingly average cookie. Serve these at your next cocktail party for a sweet surprise.

Make-Ahead Tip:
Cookie dough can be made in advance and kept refrigerated for up to 1 week or frozen for up to 1 month.

COOKIES

2 cups all-purpose flour*	4 tablespoons dark rum
½ teaspoon baking powder	2 teaspoons pure peppermint extract
¼ teaspoon salt	2 tablespoons lime zest (about 2 or 3
¾ cup vegan margarine	limes)
1 cup powdered sugar	¾ cup semisweet chocolate chips
½ cup brown sugar	(dairy-free)

TOPPING (optional)

½ cup granulated sugar	Zest of 1 lime

To make the cookies: Preheat oven to 350 degrees. Line 2 or 3 large baking sheets with parchment paper or Silpat.

In a medium bowl, whisk together flour, baking powder, and salt.

Using a stand or hand mixer, beat margarine until light and fluffy. Add powdered sugar, brown sugar, rum, and mint extract, and beat until combined. Mix in the flour mixture ½ cup at a time, then add zest and chocolate chips. Mix until combined.

To make the topping: Combine sugar and lime zest in a small bowl.

---

*For a gluten-free alternative, substitute gluten-free all-purpose flour plus ½ teaspoon xanthan gum and see page 11.

To bake the cookies: Scoop about 1 rounded tablespoon of dough at a time, and roll each scoop in the topping. Place on the prepared baking sheets, dome side up, leaving about 2 inches between each scoop. For crisper cookies, gently flatten the dough with the palm of your hand. For softer cookies, leave the scoop as is. Bake for about 12 minutes, or until the edges are lightly browned. Let cool on the pan.

Double-Chocolate Macadamia Cookies

MAKES ABOUT SIXTY-FIVE 2-INCH COOKIES

If you think there's such a thing as too much chocolate, turn the page. These chocolate-on-chocolate cookies have crisp edges, fudgy centers, and pieces of buttery macadamia nuts for a little crunch. They are rich, indulgent, and chocolaty to the max!

Make-Ahead Tip:
Cookie dough can be made in advance and kept refrigerated for up to 1 week or frozen for up to 1 month.

2¼ cups all-purpose flour*
½ cup unsweetened cocoa powder
1 tablespoon cornstarch or arrowroot
1 teaspoon baking soda
¾ teaspoon salt
¾ cup vegan margarine
1 cup brown sugar

1 cup sugar
¼ cup water
1 tablespoon pure vanilla extract
1¾ cups semisweet chocolate chips
   (dairy-free)
1 cup chopped macadamia nuts

Preheat the oven to 350 degrees. Line 2 or 3 large baking sheets with parchment paper or Silpat.

In a medium bowl, whisk flour, cocoa powder, cornstarch, baking soda, and salt until combined. Set aside.

Using a stand or hand mixer, beat the margarine, brown sugar, sugar, water, and vanilla until fluffy. Slowly beat in the flour mixture. Once the flour mixture is incorporated, add chocolate chips and macadamia nuts. Scoop about 1 rounded tablespoon of dough at a time onto the prepared baking sheets, leaving about 2 inches between each scoop. Bake for 10 to 12 minutes. Let cool on the pan.

*For a gluten-free alternative, substitute gluten-free all-purpose flour plus ½ teaspoon xanthan gum and see page 11.

Chewy Ginger-Molasses Cookies

MAKES ABOUT THIRTY-FOUR 2½-INCH COOKIES

These Chewy Ginger-Molasses Cookies have the perfect balance of sugar and spice. Molasses gives them soft and chewy centers, which I prefer over traditional crunchy ginger snaps. Plus, ginger aids in digestion, making these the perfect after-dinner cookies!

Make-Ahead Tip:
Cookie dough can be made in advance and kept refrigerated for up to 1 week or frozen for up to 1 month.

2 cups all-purpose flour*	½ teaspoon ground cloves
1 teaspoon baking soda	½ cup vegan margarine
1 teaspoon baking powder	¾ cup sugar, plus extra for rolling
1½ teaspoons ground ginger	½ cup molasses
1 teaspoon ground cinnamon	1 tablespoon water
½ teaspoon ground nutmeg	

Preheat the oven to 350 degrees. Line 2 or 3 large baking sheets with parchment paper or Silpat.

In a medium bowl, whisk together flour, baking soda, baking powder, ginger, cinnamon, nutmeg, and cloves. Set aside.

Using a stand or hand mixer, beat margarine, sugar, molasses, and water until well combined. Slowly beat in the flour mixture. Scoop about 1 rounded tablespoon of dough at a time, and roll the domed part of each scoop in sugar. Place them onto the prepared baking sheets and bake for 10 to 12 minutes. Let cool on the pan.

*For a gluten-free alternative, substitute gluten-free all-purpose flour plus ½ teaspoon xanthan gum and see page 11.

Sugar Cookies

When I have something on my mind, I like to decorate cookies. It's a creative form of self-expression, and I think the world would be a better place if everyone could turn to cookie decorating in times of emotional stress. This is my go-to recipe for classic sugar cookies, so eat 'em straight or decorate to your heart's content!

Make-Ahead Tip:
Unrolled cookie dough can be made in advance and kept refrigerated for up to 1 week or frozen for up to 1 month. Thaw before rolling out or scooping.

2½ cups all-purpose flour*
1 cup sugar, plus extra for sprinkling
½ teaspoon baking soda
1 cup vegan margarine

3 to 4 tablespoons water
1 teaspoon pure vanilla extract
Cookie Icing (page 238), optional

Preheat oven to 350 degrees. Line 2 or 3 large baking sheets with parchment paper or Silpat.

In a food processor, combine flour, 1 cup sugar, and baking soda. Add margarine, 3 tablespoons water, and vanilla. Pulse until soft and doughy. If needed, add 1 more tablespoon water.

Working with half the dough at a time, on a lightly floured surface, roll the dough out until it is ¼ inch thick. Using a 3-inch cookie cutter, cut out as many shapes as you can. You can combine any remaining scraps to roll and cut more cookies. If the dough gets too soft to work with, refrigerate it for 10 to 15 minutes.

Place the shapes on the prepared baking sheets about ½ inch apart and sprinkle with sugar. Bake for 10 to 12 minutes until lightly golden around the edges. Let cool on the pan.

When cookies have cooled completely, decorate with icing, if using, and serve.

*For a gluten-free alternative, substitute gluten-free all-purpose flour plus ½ teaspoon xanthan gum and see page 11.

Snowball Cookies

I call these snowball cookies because they are little domes of shortbread goodness, studded with chocolate chips and dusted in powdered sugar. Let it snow!

¾ cup vegan margarine

1½ cups all-purpose flour

½ cup powdered sugar, plus extra for dusting

2 teaspoons pure vanilla extract

¼ teaspoon salt

1 cup semisweet chocolate chips (dairy-free)

Preheat oven to 350 degrees. Line 2 or 3 large baking sheets with parchment paper or Silpat.

Using a stand or hand mixer, beat the margarine until fluffy. Add flour, ½ cup powdered sugar, vanilla, and salt and beat until incorporated. Add chocolate chips. Scoop about 1 rounded tablespoon of dough at a time onto the prepared baking sheets, leaving about 2 inches between each scoop. Bake for about 12 minutes until lightly golden around the edges. Remove from oven and sift powdered sugar over hot cookies. Let cool and dust with powdered sugar again before serving.

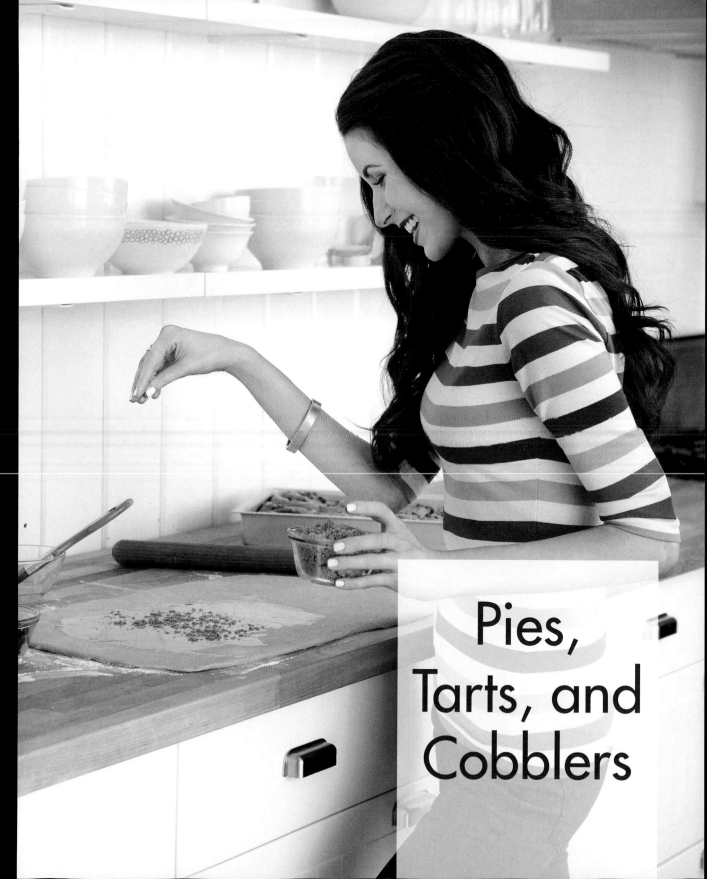

Pies,
Tarts, and
Cobblers

Easy Apple Pie

MAKES ONE 9-INCH PIE

This apple pie recipe was the treasure of my college apartment. All six of us girls had it memorized and, almost every week, a different girl was pulling a fresh, hot apple pie out of our little oven. We always kept a stash of store-bought piecrusts on hand for those cold Berkeley nights when we needed apple pie. We've all moved our separate ways, but my roommates still call me to tell me they're making the pie. Can we say Sisterhood of the Traveling Apple Pie?

½ cup sugar, plus extra for sprinkling
2 tablespoons all-purpose flour
1 teaspoon ground cinnamon
5 or 6 apples, peeled and thinly sliced

1 recipe Double Piecrust (page 242) or 2 store-bought piecrusts
Soy, almond, or rice milk for brushing

Preheat oven to 375 degrees. Lightly grease a 9-inch pie pan.

Whisk together ½ cup sugar, flour, and cinnamon in a large bowl. Add apples and mix with a large spoon until apples are evenly coated.

Remove the double piecrust dough from the refrigerator. If the dough is difficult to roll, let it soften at room temperature until it is easier to work with. On a lightly floured surface, roll out 1 disc of dough until it is about ⅛ inch thick. Carefully lift the dough and fit it into the prepared pan, letting about 1 inch hang over the sides. Fill the pie shell with the apple filling.

On a lightly floured surface, roll out the second disc of dough until it is about ⅛ inch thick. Lay it over the top of the apples and tuck excess and overhanging dough into the pie shell. Crimp the dough between your two index fingers to make a decorative border. Cut slits in the top layer of dough.

Brush the top and edges of the piecrust with nondairy milk and sprinkle with sugar for an extra-sweet and crisp top. Bake for 50 to 55 minutes, until the crust is nicely browned.

Absolutely Perfect Pumpkin Pie

MAKES ONE 9-INCH PIE

I've eaten many vegan pumpkin pies over the years, but this pie takes the cake. If you are looking for the perfect pumpkin pie recipe, one that is extremely traditional in flavor and texture, you've just found it!

Note: The pie will need to chill in the refrigerator for 4 hours or overnight before serving. Do not freeze.

1 (15-ounce) can pumpkin puree
1¼ cups canned coconut milk, mixed
    well before measuring
1 cup sugar
6 tablespoons cornstarch
2 teaspoons pure vanilla extract
½ teaspoon salt

1 teaspoon ground cinnamon
½ teaspoon ground ginger
¼ teaspoon ground nutmeg
¼ teaspoon ground cloves
1 recipe Single Piecrust (page 241)
    or 1 store-bought piecrust*
Coconut Whipped Cream (page 234)

Preheat the oven to 350 degrees. Lightly grease a 9-inch pie pan.

In a blender, combine pumpkin puree, coconut milk, sugar, cornstarch, vanilla, salt, cinnamon, ginger, nutmeg, and cloves. Process until smooth.

Remove the single piecrust dough from the refrigerator. If the dough is difficult to roll, let it soften at room temperature until it is easier to work with. On a lightly floured surface, roll out the dough until it is about ⅛-inch thick. Carefully lift the dough and fit it into the prepared pan. Trim overhanging dough using scissors or a sharp knife and reserve scraps for decorative leaves (see Tip, page 98). Fill the pie shell with the pumpkin mixture until it almost reaches the top. Bake for 60 minutes, keeping in mind that the center will not be completely set when done. If the piecrust edges brown too quickly, loosely wrap a piece of foil (about 25 inches long) around the rim. Let the finished pie cool completely, then chill in the refrigerator for 4 hours or overnight before serving. Slice and serve with a dollop of Coconut Whipped Cream.

*For a gluten-free alternative, substitute Gluten-Free Piecrust (page 243) and see page 11.

Chloe's Tip: Decorative Piecrust Leaves

To make decorative piecrust leaves, roll out reserved piecrust dough scraps and cut out leaves with a small knife. Bake on a baking sheet for 10 to 15 minutes until golden, and let cool. Arrange the leaves on top of the pie.

Chocolate Chip Cookie Pie

MAKES ONE 9-INCH PIE

This has all the flavors of a warm chocolate chip cookie in a moist chocolaty pie. Beware, this pie is super rich and decadent so start with a small piece. Extra credit if you serve it with a scoop of Vanilla Ice Cream (page 237).

Make-Ahead Tip:
Assembled, unbaked pie can be covered with plastic wrap and refrigerated overnight. Bake fresh the next day before serving.

1 recipe Single Piecrust (page 241),
    or 1 store-bought piecrust
¾ cup all-purpose flour
⅓ cup sugar
½ cup brown sugar
1 teaspoon baking powder

½ cup melted vegan margarine
¼ cup soy, almond, or rice milk
1 teaspoon pure vanilla extract
¾ cup chopped walnuts
¾ cup semisweet chocolate chips
    (dairy-free)

Preheat oven to 350 degrees. Lightly grease a 9 inch pie pan.

Remove the piecrust dough from the refrigerator. If the dough is difficult to roll, let it soften at room temperature until it is easier to work with, usually 10 to 20 minutes. On a lightly floured surface, roll out the dough until it is about ⅛-inch thick. Carefully lift the dough and fit it into the prepared pan. Trim overhanging dough using scissors or a sharp knife. Store in refrigerator while preparing the filling.

In a large bowl, whisk together flour, sugar, brown sugar, and baking powder. In a separate bowl, whisk together melted margarine, nondairy milk, and vanilla. Pour the wet mixture into the dry mixture and whisk until just combined. Fold in walnuts and chocolate chips.

Pour the filling into the prepared piecrust and bake for 50 to 55 minutes. Let cool slightly before serving.

Peach Cobbler

SERVES 6

I use this easy cobbler recipe whenever I'm having friends over. You can bake it in a large pan or bake individual servings in ramekins. I love peach cobbler, but you can use any fruit or berry (fresh or frozen) that you have on hand!

DOUGH

1⅓ cups all-purpose flour

2 tablespoons sugar, plus extra
    for sprinkling

1½ teaspoons baking powder

½ teaspoon salt

¼ cup canola oil or vegan
    margarine

½ cup soy, almond, or rice milk,
    plus extra for brushing

FRUIT

½ cup sugar

2 tablespoons all-purpose flour

1 teaspoon ground cinnamon

5 fresh peaches, peeled, pitted,
    and sliced (or about 16 ounces
    frozen peaches)

To make the dough: In a medium bowl, whisk together flour, sugar, baking powder, and salt. In a separate small bowl, whisk the oil and nondairy milk, and add it to the flour mixture. Mix with a wooden spoon until combined and it is sticky and doughy. Do not overmix.

To prepare the fruit: In a medium bowl, whisk together sugar, flour, and cinnamon. Add peaches and toss with a large spoon until the fruit is coated with the sugar mixture.

To assemble and bake the cobbler: Preheat the oven to 375 degrees.

Pour the peaches into an 8- or 9-inch baking pan or distribute evenly into 6 ramekins. Using a tablespoon, scoop lumps of dough on top of the peaches. Brush the top of the dough with nondairy milk and generously sprinkle with sugar. Bake for 45 minutes or until dough is thoroughly cooked and lightly browned on top. Be sure to rotate after 20 minutes, so that it bakes evenly.

Banana Bread Cobbler

This one tastes even better than it sounds and is even easier than it looks! When my mom first made it for me, I devoured half the pan within minutes. To call this addictive would be an understatement. Don't invite too many friends over for this one, because you're not gonna want to share!

STREUSEL TOPPING

1 cup rolled oats	½ cup all-purpose flour
¾ cup brown sugar	½ cup vegan margarine, softened

COBBLER

1 cup all-purpose flour	1 cup soy, almond, or rice milk
⅔ cup sugar	½ cup vegan margarine, melted
1½ teaspoons baking powder	3 ripe bananas, sliced
½ teaspoon salt	

Vanilla Ice Cream (page 237), optional,
for serving

Preheat the oven to 375 degrees. Lightly grease an 8-inch square pan.

To make the streusel topping: In a medium bowl, mix oats, sugar, flour, and margarine until crumbly.

To make the cobbler: In a large bowl, whisk flour, sugar, baking powder, and salt until combined. Stir in nondairy milk and melted margarine until just combined. Do not overmix.

Pour the cobbler batter into the prepared pan and arrange banana slices on top. Cover the bananas with the streusel topping and bake until golden brown, about 40 minutes, or until a toothpick inserted in the center comes out clean with a few crumbs clinging to it. Serve warm or at room temperature with a scoop of Vanilla Ice Cream, if you'd like.

Cherry Hand Pies

Hand pies are perfect for serving at gatherings at which people have to stand and eat. No plates or forks necessary, just a big stack o' napkins! People will be eating these hand over fist. Feel free to use cherries or any small berry of your choice. You may have leftover filling, which can be frozen and used later.

½ cup sugar, plus extra for sprinkling

2 tablespoons cornstarch

⅛ teaspoon salt

2 cups fresh cherries, stemmed and pitted, or 12 ounces frozen pitted cherries, quartered

1 recipe Double Piecrust (page 242), or store-bought pie dough

All-purpose flour, for work surface

Soy, almond, or rice milk, for brushing

Preheat oven to 350 degrees. Line a large baking sheet with parchment paper or Silpat.

To make the filling, whisk ½ cup sugar, cornstarch, and salt in a large bowl. Add cherries and stir with a large spoon until cherries are evenly coated with the sugar mixture.

Remove the piecrust dough from the refrigerator. If the dough is difficult to roll, let it soften at room temperature until it is easier to work with. On a lightly floured surface, roll out each disc of dough until it is about ⅛-inch thick. Cut out 5- or 6-inch circles using a large pastry cutter or the rim of a bowl. Line the dough circles on the prepared baking sheet and fill each circle with a heaping tablespoon of cherry filling. Fold half the dough circle over the filling and press the edges together with your fingertips. You may need to seal the edges with a few drops of water. Cut a slit in each hand pie. Brush the tops of the hand pies with nondairy milk and generously sprinkle with sugar. Bake for 30 to 35 minutes, or until golden. Let cool slightly before serving.

Cranberry-Pear Pie

This naturally sweetened winter pie makes for a vibrant table centerpiece or delicious holiday gift. Don't be afraid of the balsamic vinegar—it brightens the cranberry flavor!

Make-Ahead Tip:

Filling can be made in advanced and stored in the refrigerator for up to 3 days.

2 tablespoons cornstarch or arrowroot	2 teaspoons balsamic vinegar
2 tablespoons water	1 teaspoon pure vanilla extract
12 ounces fresh or frozen cranberries	1 recipe Double Piecrust (page 242),
1 cup maple syrup	or 2 store-bought piecrusts*
2 tablespoons orange juice	Soy, almond, or rice milk for
2 pears, peeled and diced	brushing
⅛ teaspoon salt	Sugar, for sprinkling

To make the filling: In a small bowl, whisk cornstarch and water. Set aside.

In a medium saucepan, combine cranberries, maple syrup, and orange juice, and bring to a boil. Reduce heat and let simmer for about 5 to 10 minutes, or until cranberries have popped. Add pears, cornstarch mixture, and salt, and let cook a few more minutes, stirring frequently, until mixture begins to thicken. Remove from heat, stir in vinegar and vanilla, and let cool completely. Cover and refrigerate for a few hours or overnight.

To assemble and bake the pie: Preheat the oven to 350 degrees. Lightly grease a 9-inch pie pan.

Remove the piecrust dough from the refrigerator. If the dough is difficult to roll, let it soften at room temperature until it is easier to work with. On a lightly floured surface, roll out 1 disc of dough until it is about ⅛-inch thick. Carefully lift the dough and fit it into the prepared pan, letting about 1 inch hang over the sides. Fill the pie shell with the cranberry filling.

*For a gluten-free alternative, substitute Gluten-Free Piecrust (page 243) and see page 11.

On a lightly floured surface, roll out the second disc of dough until it is ⅛-inch thick. Cut out eight 1-inch strips. My lattice technique does not require any weaving. Instead, lay four strips horizontally on top of the filling, leaving about ½ to ¾ inch between strips. You may want to use a metal spatula to transfer the dough strips from your work surface to your pie. Lay the remaining four strips diagonally over the first four strips, creating a diamond shape between strips. Fold the overhanging dough over the edges of the lattice top. Crimp the dough between your two index fingers to make a decorative border.

Brush the top and edges of the piecrust with nondairy milk and sprinkle with sugar for an extra sweet and crisp top. Bake for 50 to 55 minutes, until the crust is nicely browned. If the piecrust edges brown too quickly, loosely wrap a piece of foil (about 25 inches long) around the rim. Let the finished pie cool completely, then chill in the refrigerator before serving.

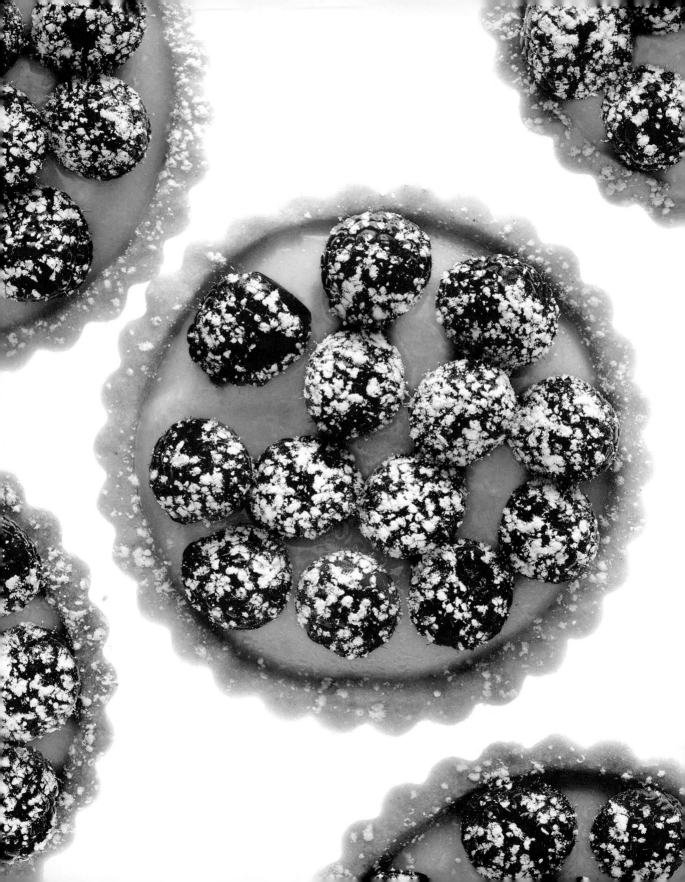

Raspberry Lemon Tart

MAKES ONE 9-INCH TART

Fresh raspberries and creamy lemon custard atop a rich shortbread crust—simple, classic, perfect. Finish with powdered sugar for an elegant presentation.

Note: The tart will need to chill in the refrigerator for 8 hours or overnight before serving.

CRUST*

1½ cups all-purpose flour	¼ teaspoon salt
⅓ cup sugar	½ cup vegan margarine

CUSTARD

¼ cup soy, almond, or rice milk	2 tablespoons lemon zest
¼ cup cornstarch or arrowroot	(about 2 lemons)
1 (13.5-ounce) can coconut milk	Natural yellow food coloring,
½ cup sugar	optional
⅛ teaspoon salt	1 pint fresh raspberries
1 teaspoon pure vanilla extract	Powdered sugar, for serving
2 teaspoons pure lemon extract	

To make the shortbread crust: Preheat the oven to 350 degrees.

In a food processor, process flour, sugar, and salt until combined. Add margarine and pulse until crumbly. Firmly press shortbread dough into a 9-inch tart pan. Bake for 20 to 25 minutes, or until edges are golden. Remove from oven and let cool completely.

To make the lemon custard: In a small bowl, thoroughly mix nondairy milk and cornstarch with a whisk or fork and set aside.

In a medium saucepan, whisk together coconut milk, sugar, and salt, and heat over medium-high heat just until boiling. Reduce heat to medium and slowly drizzle the cornstarch mixture into the saucepan, whisking continuously. Let cook until the mixture becomes very

*For a gluten-free alternative, substitute Gluten-Free Piecrust (page 243) and see page 11.

thick, like pudding, about 5 minutes, whisking frequently. Remove from heat and stir in vanilla, lemon extract, zest, and food coloring, if using.

To assemble the tart: Spread the custard evenly into the tart shell. Let cool completely, then chill it in the refrigerator for 8 hours or overnight. Garnish with raspberries and chill in the refrigerator for 8 hours or overnight. Dust with powdered sugar before serving.

Chocolate Cream Pie

MAKES ONE 9-INCH PIE

This is one of those recipes that will put your friends into total shock when they find out it's vegan. I've had friends ask me several times, "Are you sure this is vegan?" because every bite is so creamy dreamy good! For the cookie crust, pulse store-bought vegan chocolate cookies, or use the chocolate wafers from the Chloe O's recipe (page 65).

Note: The pie will need to chill in the refrigerator for 8 hours or overnight before serving.

CRUST

1½ cups chocolate cookie crumbs (dairy-free)*	¼ cup vegan margarine, melted

FILLING

¼ cup soy, almond, or rice milk	1 cup semisweet chocolate chips (dairy-free)
¼ cup cornstarch or arrowroot	
1 (13.5-ounce) can coconut milk	Coconut Whipped Cream (page 234)
½ cup sugar	
⅛ teaspoon salt	Shaved chocolate, for garnish

To make the crust: Preheat oven to 350 degrees. Lightly grease a 9-inch pie pan.

Place cookie crumbs and melted margarine in a food processor and pulse until combined. Press evenly and firmly into the prepared pie pan, spreading the crumbs up the sides. Bake for 10 minutes. Let cool completely.

To make the filling: In a small bowl, thoroughly mix nondairy milk and cornstarch with a whisk or fork and set aside.

In a medium saucepan, whisk together coconut milk, sugar, and salt, and heat over medium-high heat, just until boiling. Reduce the heat to low, and stir in chocolate chips. Let cook, whisking frequently, until completely smooth. Increase the heat to medium and slowly

*For a gluten-free alternative, use gluten-free cookies and see page 11.

drizzle the cornstarch mixture into the saucepan, whisking continuously. Let cook until the mixture becomes very thick, like pudding, 5 minutes, whisking frequently.

To assemble the pie: Pour the filling into the cookie crust. Let the pie cool completely then chill it in the refrigerator for 8 hours or overnight. Top with Coconut Whipped Cream and garnish with shaved chocolate.

Mocha Mud Pie

MAKES ONE 9-INCH PIE

My first mud pie experience was when I went on vacation to Hawaii as a little girl. I couldn't believe that ice cream could be served as a massive wedge on a plate and eaten with a fork! For the remainder of our trip, I ordered mud pie at every meal. My Mocha Mud Pie recipe is completely vegan, easy to assemble, and still has that show-stopping quality I remember. For the cookie crust, pulse store-bought vegan chocolate cookies, or use the chocolate wafers from the Chloe O's recipe (page 65).

Make-Ahead Tip:
Can be made in advance and frozen for up to 1 month. Thaw slightly before slicing.

CRUST	
1½ cups chocolate cookie crumbs (dairy-free)*	¼ cup vegan margarine, melted

FILLING	
2 pints coffee ice cream (dairy free), softened in the refrigerator for 30 minutes	Chocolate Sauce (page 232) Coconut Whipped Cream (page 234) ½ cup chopped almonds, toasted

To make the crust: Preheat oven to 350 degrees. Lightly grease a 9-inch pie pan.

Pulse the cookies in a food processor until a fine crumb has formed. Add the melted margarine and pulse until incorporated. Press evenly and firmly into the prepared pie pan, spreading the crumbs ¾ up the sides. Bake for 10 minutes. Let cool, then freeze.

To assemble the pie: Transfer the softened ice cream to a large bowl and stir with a spoon to soften even more. Spread the ice cream evenly in the chilled piecrust. Cover tightly with plastic wrap and refreeze until solid. Letting the pie sit out at room temperature for 10 minutes before serving will make it easier to slice. Slice the pie and drizzle with Chocolate Sauce, top with a dollop of Coconut Whipped Cream, and garnish with almonds.

*For a gluten-free alternative, use gluten-free cookies and see page 11.

Coconut Cream Pie

For a break from chocolate, bake yourself a Coconut Cream Pie. The luscious coconut cream filling rests delicately atop a flaky crust, making for the most perfect classic nonchocolate dessert ever!

Note: The pie will need to chill in the refrigerator for 8 hours or overnight before serving.

1 recipe Single Piecrust (page 241), or 1 store-bought piecrust*
¼ cup soy, almond, or rice milk
¼ cup cornstarch or arrowroot
1 (13.5-ounce) can coconut milk
½ cup sugar
⅛ teaspoon salt
1 teaspoon pure vanilla extract
½ cup shredded coconut
Coconut Whipped Cream (page 234)
Toasted Coconut (page 244)

Preheat oven to 350 degrees. Lightly grease a 9-inch pie pan.

Remove the piecrust dough from the refrigerator. If the dough is difficult to roll, let it soften at room temperature until it is easier to work with. On a lightly floured surface, roll out the dough until it is about ⅛-inch thick. Carefully lift the dough and fit it into the prepared pan. Trim overhanging dough using scissors or a sharp knife. Puncture the dough a few times with a fork to prevent air bubbles, and freeze for 30 minutes. Bake for about 25 minutes until the crust is lightly golden. If the edges of the crust get too dark while baking, loosely cover the edges with foil. Let the crust cool completely before filling.

Meanwhile, thoroughly mix nondairy milk and cornstarch in a small bowl with a whisk or fork. Set aside.

In a medium saucepan, whisk together coconut milk, sugar, and salt, and heat over medium-high heat just until boiling. Reduce the heat to medium and slowly drizzle the cornstarch mixture into the saucepan, whisking continuously. Let cook until the mixture becomes very thick, like pudding, about 5 minutes, whisking frequently. Remove from heat and whisk in vanilla and shredded coconut.

*For a gluten-free alternative, substitute Gluten-Free Piecrust (page 243) and see page 11.

To assemble the pie: Pour the filling into the crust. Let the pie cool completely then chill it in the refrigerator for 8 hours or overnight. Top with Coconut Whipped Cream and garnish with Toasted Coconut.

Cakes
and
Cupcakes

Spiced Applesauce Cake

Move over weird-colored fruitcake! During the holiday season, I don't leave my house without Spiced Applesauce Cake. From end-of-the-year office potlucks to family holiday parties, this cake always makes an appearance. It's very moist, subtly sweet, and perfectly spiced. Plus, Bundt cakes are super easy to transport! Top it with my sweet maple icing or simply dust powdered sugar over the top for a shortcut. To make the cake sugar free, substitute 1¼ cups pure maple syrup for the sugar.

CAKE

2¼ cups all-purpose flour*	½ cup canola oil
2 teaspoons baking soda	¼ cup white or apple-cider
1 teaspoon salt	vinegar
1½ teaspoons ground cinnamon	1 tablespoon pure vanilla
½ teaspoon ground nutmeg	extract
½ teaspoon ground ginger	½ cup raisins
2 cups unsweetened applesauce	½ cup chopped walnuts
1½ cups brown sugar	

MAPLE ICING

1½ cups powdered sugar	1 to 3 tablespoons water
3 tablespoons maple syrup	

To make the cake: Preheat the oven to 350 degrees. Lightly grease a Bundt pan.

In a large bowl, whisk together flour, baking soda, salt, cinnamon, nutmeg, and ginger. In a separate bowl, whisk together applesauce, brown sugar, oil, vinegar, and vanilla. Pour the wet mixture into the dry mixture and whisk until just combined. Do not overmix. Gently fold in raisins and walnuts (see Tip, page 122).

Fill the prepared pan evenly with batter. Bake for 40 to 45 minutes, or until a toothpick inserted in the center of the cake comes out dry with a few crumbs clinging to it. Rotate the cake halfway through baking time. Let the cake cool completely before unmolding.

*For a gluten-free alternative, substitute gluten-free all-purpose flour plus 1 teaspoon xanthan gum and see page 11.

To make the maple icing: In a medium bowl, whisk together powdered sugar, maple syrup, and 1 tablespoon water at a time, until it becomes a thick yet pourable icing.

To assemble the cake: Once the cake is completely cooled, run a knife around the inside edges of the pan to loosen. Gently unmold the cake and place on a wire rack over parchment paper or a baking sheet. For a less sweet dessert, very lightly drizzle some of the icing over the cake. If you prefer a sweeter dessert, be more generous with the icing. Regardless, you may not need to use all of the icing. Transfer to a platter and serve.

Chloe's Tip: How to Prevent Raisins from Sinking During Baking

To keep raisins, nuts, or chocolate chips from sinking to the bottom of a cake during baking, toss the add-ins in 1 tablespoon flour before adding them to your batter. This will ensure even distribution throughout the cake.

Classic Coconut Layer Cake

MAKES TWO 9-INCH ROUND LAYERS.
DOUBLE THE RECIPE FOR FOUR LAYERS.

If you love simple old-fashioned, bakery-style cakes, you will swoon for this fluffy and moist classic coconut layer cake. When I bake a spread of desserts for a crowd, this cake is always the first to go!

Make-Ahead Tip:

Cake layers can be made in advance and frozen, unfrosted, for up to 1 month. Thaw and frost before serving.

CAKE

3 cups all-purpose flour*	1 cup canola oil
2 cups sugar	¼ cup white or apple-cider
2 teaspoons baking soda	vinegar
1 teaspoon salt	2 tablespoons pure vanilla extract
2 cups soy, almond, or rice milk	1½ cups shredded coconut
Vanilla Frosting (page 239)	2 cups shredded coconut, for topping

To make the cake: Preheat the oven to 350 degrees. Lightly grease two 9-inch round cake pans and line the bottoms with parchment paper.

In a large bowl, whisk together flour, sugar, baking soda, and salt. In a separate bowl, whisk together nondairy milk, oil, vinegar, and vanilla. Pour the wet mixture into the dry mixture and whisk until just combined. Do not overmix. Gently fold in coconut.

Fill each prepared cake pan evenly with batter. Bake for 30 to 35 minutes, or until a toothpick inserted in the center of the cake comes out dry with a few crumbs clinging to it. Rotate the cakes halfway through baking time. Let the cakes cool completely before assembly.

To assemble the cake: Once the cakes have completely cooled, run a knife around the inside edge of each cake pan to loosen, and gently unmold. Peel off the parchment paper and slice

*For a gluten-free alternative, substitute gluten-free all-purpose flour plus 1½ teaspoons xanthan gum and see page 11.

the dome off the top of each cake for even assembly, if desired. Place one cake on a serving plate or cardboard cake circle, and slide strips of parchment paper under the edges of the bottom of the cake to prevent frosting from getting on the plate. Spread a generous layer of frosting on top of the cake. Place the second cake on top of the first and spread a generous layer of frosting on top. Frost the sides and sprinkle coconut over the entire cake. Remove the parchment paper before serving.

Brooklyn Blackout Cake

MAKES THREE 9-INCH ROUND LAYERS

Welcome to the dark side! Blackout cake originated in Brooklyn, at Ebinger's Bakery, and gets its name from the blackout drills performed during World War II. The whole city would dim its lights as ships sailed to war so that the enemy could not spot them. Just like the original version, this cake is filled and frosted with chocolate pudding and coated in cake crumbs.

Note: The pudding will need to chill in the refrigerator for 3 hours before frosting.

Make-Ahead Tip:
Cake layers can be made in advance and frozen, unfrosted, for up to 1 month. Pudding can be stored in the refrigerator for up to 1 week. Thaw cakes and frost before serving.

PUDDING

¼ cup cornstarch or arrowroot	⅛ teaspoon salt
¼ cup soy, almond, or rice milk	1 cup semisweet chocolate chips
1 (13.5-ounce) can coconut milk	(dairy-free)
½ cup sugar	

CAKE

3 cups all-purpose flour*	2 cups cold coffee or water
2 cups sugar	1 cup canola oil
⅔ cup unsweetened cocoa powder	¼ cup white or apple-cider vinegar
2 teaspoons baking soda	1 tablespoon pure vanilla extract
1 teaspoon salt	

To make the pudding: In a small bowl, thoroughly whisk cornstarch and nondairy milk until smooth and set aside.

In a medium saucepan, whisk coconut milk, sugar, and salt, and cook over medium-high heat until just boiling. Reduce heat to low, and stir in chocolate chips. Let cook, whisking frequently, until completely smooth. Increase heat to medium and slowly drizzle the

*For a gluten-free alternative, substitute gluten-free all-purpose flour plus 1½ teaspoons xanthan gum and see page 11.

Chloe's Vegan Desserts

cornstarch mixture into the saucepan, whisking continuously. Let cook until the mixture becomes very thick, like pudding, about 5 minutes, whisking frequently. Remove from heat and transfer to a bowl. Cover with plastic wrap, pressing the surface of the pudding with the plastic wrap to prevent a skin from forming. Let cool slightly, then chill in the refrigerator until cool to the touch, about 3 hours.

To make the cake: Preheat the oven to 350 degrees. Lightly grease two 9-inch round cake pans and line the bottoms with parchment paper.

In a large bowl, whisk together flour, sugar, cocoa, baking soda, and salt. In a separate bowl, whisk together coffee, oil, vinegar, and vanilla. Pour the wet mixture into the dry mixture and whisk until just combined. Do not overmix.

Fill each prepared cake pan evenly with batter. Bake for about 30 minutes, or until a toothpick inserted in the center of the cake comes out dry with a few crumbs clinging to it. Be sure to rotate the cakes halfway through baking time. Let the cakes cool completely before assembly.

To assemble the cake: Once the cakes are completely cooled, run a knife around the inside edge of each cake pan to loosen, and gently unmold the cake. Peel off the parchment paper and slice each layer in half horizontally, so that you have 4 layers. Break 1 layer into pieces and pulse in the food processor until crumbly. Set cake crumbs aside. You will assemble the cake with the remaining 3 layers. Place one layer on a serving plate or cardboard cake circle, and slide strips of parchment paper under the edges of the bottom of the cake to prevent frosting from getting on the plate. Spread a generous layer of pudding on top of the cake. Place another cake layer on top of the first and spread a generous layer of pudding on top. Repeat with the remaining layer. Frost the sides with pudding and sprinkle the cake crumbs over the entire cake. Remove the parchment paper before serving.

Mixed Berry Shortcake

MAKES TWO 9-INCH ROUND LAYERS.
DOUBLE THE RECIPE FOR FOUR LAYERS.

Sure, you could stick to strawberries, but I like to use an assortment of summer berries from the farmers market in my shortcake. Coconut whipped cream is an excellent substitute for traditional whipped cream because it is much lighter and more flavorful.

Make-Ahead Tip:

Cake layers can be made in advance and frozen, unfrosted, for up to 1 month. Coconut Whipped Cream can be made the day before and stored in the refrigerator. Thaw cakes and assemble before serving.

CAKE

3 cups all-purpose flour*	1 cup canola oil
2 cups sugar	¼ cup white or apple-cider
2 teaspoons baking soda	vinegar
1 teaspoon salt	2 tablespoons pure vanilla
2 cups soy, almond, or rice milk	extract

TOPPING

3 cups fresh berries (sliced strawberries, blueberries, raspberries, or blackberries)	Coconut Whipped Cream (page 234)

To make the cake: Preheat the oven to 350 degrees. Lightly grease two 9-inch round cake pans and line the bottoms with parchment paper.

In a large bowl, whisk together flour, sugar, baking soda, and salt. In a separate bowl, whisk together nondairy milk, oil, vinegar, and vanilla. Pour the wet mixture into the dry mixture and whisk until just combined. Do not overmix.

*For a gluten-free alternative, substitute gluten-free all-purpose flour plus 1½ teaspoons xanthan gum and see page 11.

Fill each prepared cake pan evenly with batter. Bake for 30 to 35 minutes, or until a toothpick inserted in the center of the cake comes out dry with a few crumbs clinging to it. Rotate the cakes halfway through baking time. Let the cakes cool completely before assembly.

To assemble the cake: Once the cakes are completely cooled, run a knife around the inside edge of each cake pan to loosen, and gently unmold the cake. Peel off the parchment paper and slice the dome off the top of each cake for even assembly, if desired. Place one cake on a serving plate or cardboard cake circle. Spread a layer of Coconut Whipped Cream on top of the cake. Arrange half the berries on top of the whipped cream. Place the second cake on top of the first and spread a layer of whipped cream on top. Arrange remaining berries on top of the cake and serve.

Chloe's Celebration Cake

MAKES TWO 9-INCH ROUND LAYERS.
DOUBLE THE RECIPE FOR FOUR LAYERS.

This is my signature cake. It's easy to decorate and extremely delicious, so I make it for every celebratory occasion. Give it a try and maybe it will become your signature cake, too!

Make-Ahead Tip:

Cake layers can be made in advance and frozen, unfrosted, for up to 1 month. Thaw cakes and frost before serving.

CAKE

3 cups all-purpose flour*	2 cups cold coffee or water
2 cups sugar	1 cup canola oil
⅔ cup unsweetened cocoa powder	¼ cup white or apple-cider
2 teaspoons baking soda	vinegar
1 teaspoon salt	1 tablespoon pure vanilla extract

Vanilla Frosting (page 239)	Powdered sugar, for serving
Fresh raspberries, for garnish	

To make the cake: Preheat the oven to 350 degrees. Lightly grease two 9-inch round cake pans and line the bottoms with parchment paper.

In a large bowl, whisk together flour, sugar, cocoa, baking soda, and salt. In a separate bowl, whisk together coffee, oil, vinegar, and vanilla. Pour the wet mixture into the dry mixture and whisk until just combined. Do not overmix.

Fill each prepared cake pan evenly with batter. Bake for about 30 minutes, or until a toothpick inserted in the center of the cake comes out dry with a few crumbs clinging to it. Be sure to rotate the cakes halfway through baking time. Let the cakes cool completely before assembly.

---

*For a gluten-free alternative, substitute gluten-free all-purpose flour plus 1½ teaspoons xanthan gum and see page 11.

To assemble the cake: Once the cakes are completely cooled, run a knife around the inside edge of each cake pan to loosen, and gently unmold the cake. Peel off the parchment paper and slice the dome off the top of each cake for even assembly, if desired. Place one cake on a serving plate or cardboard cake circle. Spread a generous layer of Vanilla Frosting on top of the cake. Place the second cake on top of the first and spread a generous layer of frosting on top. Decorate with raspberries and dust with powdered sugar immediately before serving.

Lemon Olive-Oil Cake

MAKES 1 BUNDT CAKE

Have you ever baked a cake with olive oil? It may seem strange, but in Italy they do it all the time! Extra-virgin olive oil adds a subtle depth of flavor and richness to cake, which is perfect for vegan baking. Olive oil is also a heart-healthy oil (aka "good fat") that protects against heart disease and high cholesterol. Instead of sugar, I use pure maple syrup, which is a healthier alternative and compliments the olive oil flavor nicely. So, what are you waiting for? Try this easy recipe and enjoy a piece of moist lemon cake topped with fresh berries—guilt free! For a decadent touch, top with a dollop of Coconut Whipped Cream (page 234).

2 cups all-purpose flour*
1 teaspoon baking soda
1 teaspoon baking powder
½ teaspoon salt
½ cup extra-virgin olive oil
¾ cup maple syrup
¾ cup water

¼ cup lemon juice
2 tablespoons lemon zest
   (about 2 lemons)
1 tablespoon lemon extract
Powdered sugar, for garnish
Fresh berries, for garnish

To make the cake: Preheat the oven to 350 degrees. Lightly grease a Bundt pan.

In a large bowl, whisk together flour, baking soda, baking powder, and salt. In a separate bowl, whisk together oil, maple syrup, water, lemon juice and zest, and lemon extract. Pour the wet mixture into the dry mixture and whisk until just combined. Do not overmix.

Fill the prepared Bundt pan evenly with batter. Bake for about 30 minutes, or until a toothpick inserted in the cake comes out dry with a few crumbs clinging to it. Rotate halfway through the baking time. Cool the cake completely before unmolding.

To serve: Plate a slice of cake and sift powdered sugar over the top. Garnish with fresh berries.

*For a gluten-free alternative, substitute gluten-free all-purpose flour plus 1 teaspoon xanthan gum and see page 11.

German Chocolate Cake

MAKES TWO 9-INCH ROUND LAYERS.
DOUBLE THE RECIPE FOR FOUR LAYERS.

This one is for the men! Both my dad and grandpa are German-Chocolate-Cake-aholics, and request it each year on their birthdays. Once I showed up at my grandpa's birthday party with this cake, not knowing that there was already a table full of German Chocolate Cakes that many others had brought him. To my surprise, my vegan cake was the favorite of the party!

Make-Ahead Tip:
Cake layers can be made in advance and frozen, unfrosted, for up to 1 month. Filling can be stored in the refrigerator for up to 1 week. Thaw cakes and frost before serving.

FILLING

¼ cup cornstarch or arrowroot

3 tablespoons water

1 (13.5-ounce) can coconut milk

1¾ cups brown sugar

1 tablespoon pure vanilla extract

1 cup chopped toasted pecans

4 cups shredded coconut

CAKE

3 cups all-purpose flour*

2 cups sugar

⅓ cup unsweetened cocoa powder

2 teaspoons baking soda

1 teaspoon salt

2 cups canned coconut milk,
mixed well before measuring

1 cup canola oil

¼ cup white or apple-cider
vinegar

1 tablespoon pure vanilla
extract

To make the filling: In a small bowl, thoroughly whisk cornstarch and water until smooth and set aside.

In a medium saucepan, whisk coconut milk and brown sugar, and cook over medium-high heat until just boiling. Reduce heat to medium and slowly drizzle the cornstarch mixture

*For a gluten-free alternative, substitute gluten-free all-purpose flour plus 1½ teaspoons xanthan gum and see page 11.

into the saucepan, whisking continuously. Let cook until the mixture becomes very thick, like pudding, about 5 minutes, whisking frequently. Remove from heat and fold in vanilla, pecans, and coconut flakes. Let cool slightly, then chill in the refrigerator until cool to the touch, about 3 hours.

To make the cake: Preheat the oven to 350 degrees. Lightly grease two 9-inch round cake pans and line the bottoms with parchment paper.

In a large bowl, whisk together flour, sugar, cocoa, baking soda, and salt. In a separate bowl, whisk together coconut milk, oil, vinegar, and vanilla. Pour the wet mixture into the dry mixture and whisk until just combined. Do not overmix.

Fill each prepared cake pan evenly with batter. Bake for about 30 minutes, or until a toothpick inserted in the center of the cake comes out dry with a few crumbs clinging to it. Be sure to rotate the cakes halfway through baking time. Let the cakes cool completely before assembly.

To assemble the cake: Once the cakes are completely cooled, run a knife around the inside edge of each cake pan to loosen, and gently unmold the cake. Peel off the parchment paper and slice the dome off the top of each cake for even assembly, if desired. Place one cake on a serving plate or cardboard cake circle. Spread a generous layer of filling on top of the cake. Place the second cake on top of the first and spread a generous layer of filling on top. Frost the sides, if desired, and serve.

Chloe's Vegan Desserts

Banana Blueberry Cake with Lemon Buttercream

MAKES TWO 9-INCH ROUND LAYERS.
DOUBLE THE RECIPE FOR FOUR LAYERS.

Moist banana cake dotted with juicy blueberries and filled with sweet lemon buttercream—berries 'n' cream bliss! This light and refreshing flavor combination is always a hit at my summer dinner parties.

Make-Ahead Tip:

Cake layers can be made in advance and frozen, unfrosted, for up to 1 month. Frosting can be made the day before and stored at room temperature. Thaw cakes and frost before serving.

CAKE

2 cups all-purpose flour*
1 cup sugar
1 teaspoon baking powder
½ teaspoon baking soda
1 teaspoon salt
½ teaspoon ground cinnamon
½ teaspoon ground nutmeg
½ teaspoon ground cloves
½ teaspoon ground ginger

1 cup mashed bananas (about 2 or 3 very ripe bananas mashed on a plate using the back of a fork)
1 cup canned coconut milk, mixed well before measuring
½ cup canola oil
1 tablespoon white or apple-cider vinegar
1 tablespoon pure vanilla extract
1½ cups fresh or frozen blueberries, plus extra for garnish

BUTTERCREAM

1 cup non-hydrogenated vegetable shortening
3 cups powdered sugar

1 tablespoon lemon zest
3 to 5 tablespoons lemon juice

*For a gluten-free alternative, substitute gluten-free all-purpose flour plus 1 teaspoon xanthan gum and see page 11.

To make the cake: Preheat the oven to 350 degrees. Lightly grease two 9-inch round cake pans and line the bottoms with parchment paper.

In a large bowl, whisk together flour, sugar, baking powder, baking soda, salt, cinnamon, nutmeg, cloves, and ginger. In a separate bowl, whisk together bananas, coconut milk, oil, vinegar, and vanilla. Pour the wet mixture into the dry mixture and whisk until just combined. Do not overmix. Gently fold in 1½ cups blueberries.

Fill each prepared cake pan evenly with batter. Bake for 32 to 35 minutes, or until a toothpick inserted in the center of the cake comes out dry with a few crumbs clinging to it. Rotate the cakes halfway through baking time. Let the cakes cool completely before assembly.

To make the buttercream: Using a stand or hand mixer, beat shortening until smooth. With the mixer running on low, add powdered sugar, lemon zest, and 1 tablespoon lemon juice at a time, as needed, until frosting reaches a spreadable consistency. Increase the speed to high and beat for 2 more minutes until light and fluffy.

To assemble the cake: Once the cakes are completely cooled, run a knife around the inside edge of each cake pan to loosen, and gently unmold the cake. Peel off the parchment paper and slice the dome off the top of each cake for even assembly, if desired. Place one cake on a serving plate or cardboard cake circle. Spread a generous layer of frosting on top of the cake. Place the second cake on top of the first and spread a generous layer of frosting on top. Garnish with fresh blueberries, if desired, and serve.

Hot-Fudge-on-the-Bottom Cake

MAKES ONE 8-INCH SQUARE PAN

So, you've never baked a cake before? Try Hot-Fudge-on-the-Bottom Cake and you'll feel like a pro! This ooey-gooey chocolate cake is easy, quick, and foolproof. It's served straight from the pan with no unmolding or decorating needed. Plus, you don't even have to make a separate frosting because of the hot fudge layer that forms on the bottom. Sweet deal, don't you think?

CAKE LAYER

1 cup all-purpose flour*	¼ teaspoon salt
¾ cup sugar	½ cup soy, almond, or rice
2 tablespoons unsweetened cocoa	milk
powder	3 tablespoons canola oil
2 teaspoons baking powder	1 teaspoon pure vanilla extract

FUDGE LAYER

¼ cup brown sugar	¼ cup unsweetened cocoa powder
½ cup sugar	1½ cups boiling water

To make the cake layer: Preheat the oven to 350 degrees. Lightly grease an 8-inch square cake pan.

In a large bowl, whisk together flour, sugar, cocoa, baking powder, and salt. In a separate bowl, whisk together nondairy milk, oil, and vanilla. Pour the wet mixture into the dry mixture and whisk until just combined. Do not overmix. Spread batter into the prepared pan.

To make the fudge layer: In a small bowl, whisk together brown sugar, sugar, and cocoa. Sprinkle this mixture over the cake batter in pan. Slowly pour boiling water evenly over the batter. Do not stir.

Bake for 45 minutes. Let cool for 25 minutes before serving.

*For a gluten-free alternative, substitute gluten-free all-purpose flour plus ½ teaspoon xanthan gum and see page 11.

Vanilla Birthday Cupcakes

MAKES 14 CUPCAKES

Everyone loves a classic bakery-style birthday cupcake. If I'm baking for kids, I like to decorate these with colored sprinkles. For a more elegant and adult look, try garnishing with edible flowers!

Make-Ahead Tip:
Cupcakes can be made in advance and frozen, unfrosted, for up to 1 month. Thaw cupcakes and frost before serving.

1½ cups all-purpose flour★
1 cup sugar
1 teaspoon baking soda
½ teaspoon salt
¾ cup soy, almond, or rice milk

½ cup canola oil
2 tablespoons white or apple-cider
   vinegar
1 tablespoon pure vanilla extract

Vanilla Frosting (page 239)
Pink or red natural food coloring,
   optional

Sprinkles, optional

To make the cupcakes: Preheat the oven to 350 degrees. Line a 12-cup cupcake pan with cupcake liners.

In a large bowl, whisk together flour, sugar, baking soda, and salt. In a separate bowl, whisk together nondairy milk, oil, vinegar, and vanilla. Pour the wet mixture into the dry mixture and whisk until just combined. Do not overmix.

Fill the cupcake liners about two-thirds full with batter. Bake for about 18 to 20 minutes, or until a toothpick inserted in the center of the cupcake comes out dry with a few crumbs clinging to it. Let the cupcakes cool completely before frosting.

★For a gluten-free alternative, substitute gluten-free all-purpose flour plus ¾ teaspoon xanthan gum and see page 11.

To assemble the cupcakes: In a small bowl, mix vanilla frosting with a drop or two of food coloring until desired color is achieved. Pipe or spread a layer frosting on the cupcakes and decorate with sprinkles, if desired.

Dark Chocolate Fudge Cake

MAKES TWO 9-INCH ROUND LAYERS

I'm a bit of a traditionalist when it comes to chocolate cake. Sure, fancy decorations and flavor twists are fun once in awhile, but sometimes I just want to curl up on the couch with a cup of coffee and slab of old-fashioned chocolate layer cake. This recipe yields an extremely moist, dark, and fudgy cake, which is just how I like it.

Make-Ahead Tip:
Cake layers can be made in advance and frozen, unfrosted, for up to 1 month. Thaw cakes and frost before serving.

CAKE

1¾ cups all-purpose flour*

1¾ cups sugar

¾ cup unsweetened cocoa powder

½ teaspoon baking soda

1 teaspoon baking powder

1 teaspoon salt

1 cup canned coconut milk, mixed well before measuring

½ cup canola oil

2 tablespoons white or apple-cider vinegar

1 teaspoon pure vanilla extract

1 cup fresh hot coffee

Fudge Frosting (page 240)

To make the cake: Preheat the oven to 350 degrees. Lightly grease two 9-inch round cake pans and line the bottoms with parchment paper.

In a large bowl, whisk together flour, sugar, cocoa, baking soda, baking powder, and salt. In a separate bowl, whisk together coconut milk, oil, vinegar, and vanilla. Pour the wet mixture into the dry mixture and add hot coffee. Whisk until just combined. Do not overmix.

Fill each prepared cake pan evenly with batter. Bake for 30 to 35 minutes, or until a toothpick inserted in the center of the cake comes out dry with a few crumbs clinging to it. Be

*For a gluten-free alternative, substitute gluten-free all-purpose flour plus ¾ teaspoon xanthan gum and see page 11.

sure to rotate the cakes halfway through baking time. Let the cakes cool completely before assembly, or else the cakes will fall apart.

To assemble the cake: Once the cakes are completely cooled, run a knife around the inside edge of each cake pan to loosen, and gently unmold the cake. Peel off the parchment paper. Place one cake on a serving plate or cardboard cake circle. Spread a generous layer of frosting on top of the cake. Place the second cake on top of the first and spread a generous layer of frosting on top. Frost sides, if desired, and serve.

Yoga Cupcakes

In my first book, Chloe's Kitchen, *I feature my favorite after-yoga treat: yoga cookies. The response was so huge from yogis and chefs around the world that I decided to share my yoga cupcakes in this book! At only 113 calories each, these cupcakes are chocolaty, indulgent, and guilt-free, for a post-yoga dessert. Plus, these low-cal cupcakes taste much better than the processed diet desserts in the frozen foods section of your grocery store. So hit the mat and eat up!*

Make-Ahead Tip:

Cupcakes can be made in advance and frozen, unfrosted, for up to 1 month. Thaw cupcakes and frost before serving.

CUPCAKES

1½ cups all-purpose flour*	½ cup canola oil
1 cup sugar	2 tablespoons white or apple-
⅓ cup unsweetened cocoa powder	cider vinegar
1 teaspoon baking soda	1 tablespoon pure vanilla
½ teaspoon salt	extract
1 cup water	

FROSTING

1 cup semisweet chocolate chips (dairy-free)	3 tablespoons soy, almond, or rice milk
	Fresh raspberries, for garnish

To make the cupcakes: Preheat the oven to 350 degrees. Line two 24-cup mini cupcake pans with 34 mini cupcake liners.

In a large bowl, whisk together flour, sugar, cocoa, baking soda, and salt. In a separate bowl, whisk together water, oil, vinegar, and vanilla. Pour the wet mixture into the dry mixture and whisk until just combined. Do not overmix.

---

*For a gluten-free alternative, substitute gluten-free all-purpose flour plus ¾ teaspoon xanthan gum and see page 11.

Fill the cupcake liners about two-thirds full with batter. Bake for 12 to 15 minutes, or until a toothpick inserted in the center of the cupcake comes out dry, with a few crumbs clinging to it. Cool the cupcakes completely before frosting.

To make the frosting: Melt the chocolate chips and nondairy milk in a double boiler or microwave. Whisk until smooth. Spread a thin layer of frosting on each chocolate cupcake and top with 1 fresh raspberry.

Salted Caramel Cupcakes

MAKES 12 CUPCAKES

Salted caramel is all the rage right now and I can see why! For those of us who can't decide between sweet and salty, this cupcake solves the problem.

Make-Ahead Tip:

Cupcakes can be made in advance and frozen, unfrosted, for up to 1 month. Frosting should be made fresh. Thaw cupcakes and frost before serving.

CUPCAKES

1½ cups all-purpose flour*	½ cup canola oil
1 cup sugar	2 tablespoons white or apple-
1 teaspoon baking soda	cider vinegar
½ teaspoon salt	1 tablespoon pure vanilla extract
¾ cup soy, almond, or rice milk	

FROSTING

½ cup vegan margarine	¼ teaspoon salt
1 cup dark brown sugar	1 teaspoon pure vanilla extract
¼ cup soy, almond, or rice milk, plus	3 cups powdered sugar
more as needed	Fleur de sel, for sprinkling

To make the cupcakes: Preheat the oven to 350 degrees. Line a 12-cup cupcake pan with cupcake liners.

In a large bowl, whisk together flour, sugar, baking soda, and salt. In a separate bowl, whisk together nondairy milk, oil, vinegar, and vanilla. Pour the wet mixture into the dry mixture and whisk until just combined. Do not overmix.

Fill the cupcake liners about two-thirds full with batter. Bake for about 20 minutes, or until a toothpick inserted in the center of the cupcake comes out dry with a few crumbs clinging to it. Let the cupcakes cool completely before frosting.

*For a gluten-free alternative, substitute gluten-free all-purpose flour plus ¾ teaspoon xanthan gum and see page 11.

To make the frosting: In a medium saucepan, melt margarine and whisk in brown sugar, non-dairy milk, and salt. Bring to a gentle boil, and let boil for 3 to 4 minutes. Remove from heat, stir in vanilla, and let cool.

Using a stand or hand mixer, slowly beat the caramel mixture with powdered sugar. If frosting is too thick, add 1 tablespoon nondairy milk at a time, until frosting reaches a spreadable consistency. Beat on high until smooth.

To assemble the cupcakes: Spread a thin layer of frosting on the cupcakes and sprinkle with a few flakes of fleur de sel.

Chloe's Award-Winning Chocolate Orange Cupcakes with Candied Orange Peel

MAKES 14 CUPCAKES

Chocolate and orange is the world's best-kept-flavor-combo secret! It is rarely used, but it is so simple and decadent. When I competed on Food Network's Cupcake Wars, *pitted against three nonvegan bakers to fight for the cupcake crown, I knew I needed to use flavors that would stand out. I came up with these Chocolate Orange Cupcakes, which are filled with orange buttercream, topped with slick chocolate ganache, and adorned with sweet 'n' tangy candied orange peels. This recipe earned me top prize and the judges devoured every last chocolaty orange crumb. One of the judges, Candace Nelson of Sprinkles Cupcakes, even said that chocolate and orange is her favorite combo, too!*

Make-Ahead Tip:
Cupcakes can be made in advance and frozen, unfrosted, for up to 1 month. Candied orange peels can be stored in the freezer for up to 3 months and Orange Buttercream can be made the day before and stored at room temperature. Thaw cupcakes and assemble before serving.

CANDIED ORANGE PEELS

1 orange	¾ cup sugar, divided
1¾ cups water, divided	

CUPCAKES

1½ cups all-purpose flour*	¾ cup orange juice
1 cup sugar	½ cup canola oil
½ cup unsweetened cocoa powder	1 tablespoon white or apple cider
1 teaspoon baking powder	vinegar
½ teaspoon baking soda	1 teaspoon pure vanilla extract
¼ teaspoon salt	Zest of 1 orange

*For a gluten-free alternative, substitute gluten-free all-purpose flour plus ¾ teaspoon xanthan gum and see page 11.

½ cup non-hydrogenated vegetable
    shortening
1½ cups powdered sugar

2 tablespoons orange juice
1 teaspoon pure orange extract,
    optional

GANACHE

1 cup semisweet chocolate chips
    (dairy-free)
¼ cup canned coconut milk,
    mixed well before measuring

2 tablespoons canola oil
1 teaspoon pure orange extract,
    optional

To make the candied orange peels: Using a vegetable peeler, peel thin slices of orange peel from an orange. Depending on the size of your peeler, you may want to cut the slices even thinner using a knife. In a small saucepan, combine the orange peels and ½ cup water. Bring to a boil and let cook for 5 minutes. Drain the water, place the peels back in the pot, and refill with ½ cup water. Bring the water to a boil again, let cook for 5 minutes, and drain. Repeat this process one more time to release the bitterness from the orange peels.

Bring ¼ cup sugar, ¼ cup of water, and the orange peels to a boil and let cook on medium-high heat until the liquid bubbles away. Remove from heat; spread out to cool on parchment paper. Once the candied peels are somewhat dried (about 10 minutes), roll them in the remaining sugar until thoroughly coated. Store in refrigerator or freezer.

To make the cupcakes: Preheat the oven to 350 degrees. Line two 12-cup cupcake pans with 14 cupcake liners.

In a large bowl, whisk together flour, sugar, cocoa, baking powder, baking soda, and salt. In a separate bowl, whisk together orange juice, oil, vinegar, vanilla, and zest. Pour the wet mixture into the dry mixture and whisk until just combined. Do not overmix. The batter will be thick.

Fill the cupcake liners about two-thirds full with batter. Bake for 16 to 20 minutes, or until a toothpick inserted in the center of the cupcake comes out dry with a few crumbs clinging to it. Let the cupcakes cool completely before frosting.

To make the buttercream: Using a stand or hand mixer, beat shortening until smooth. With the mixer running on low, add powdered sugar and orange juice, a little at a time, as needed,

until frosting reaches a spreadable consistency. Add orange extract, if using. Increase the speed to high and beat for 2 more minutes until light and fluffy.

To make the ganache: Melt chocolate chips and coconut milk in a double boiler or microwave. Whisk in oil and orange extract, if using, until smooth.

To assemble the cupcakes: Fit a piping bag with a small round or Bismarck tip and fill with the orange buttercream. Insert the tip into the center of the top of each cupcake and squeeze the bag to fill the cupcake with about 2 to 3 teaspoons of buttercream. There is no need to scoop out any of the cake. Spread the top of each cupcake with a thin layer of chocolate ganache and garnish with candied orange peels.

Mint Cookies 'n' Cream Cupcakes

MAKES 16 CUPCAKES

This cupcake has some serious crunch factor. The cookie pieces in the batter and frosting keep you on your toes at every bite! A hint of mint kicks up the flavor and keeps it refreshing. Feel free to use store-bought vegan sandwich cookies, from brands such as Newman O's or Whole Foods, or use Chloe O's (page 65).

Make-Ahead Tip:

Cupcakes can be made in advance and frozen, unfrosted, for up to 1 month. Frosting can be made the day before and stored at room temperature. Thaw cupcakes and frost before serving.

CUPCAKES

1½ cups all-purpose flour*	2 tablespoons white or apple-cider
1 cup sugar	vinegar
⅓ cup unsweetened cocoa powder	1 tablespoon pure vanilla extract
1 teaspoon baking soda	1 cup crushed store-bought
½ teaspoon salt	chocolate sandwich cookies
1 cup cold coffee or water	(dairy-free)
½ cup canola oil	

FROSTING

1 cup non-hydrogenated vegetable shortening	3 to 5 tablespoons soy, almond, or rice milk
2 cups powdered sugar	2 cups crushed store-bought
1 teaspoon pure peppermint extract	chocolate sandwich cookies (dairy-free)
	Fresh Mint, for garnish

To make the cupcakes: Preheat the oven to 350 degrees. Line two 12-cup cupcake pans with 16 cupcake liners.

---

*For gluten-free cupcakes, substitute gluten-free all-purpose flour plus ¾ teaspoon xanthan gum and see page 11. Also, use gluten-free cookies in the cupcakes and frosting.

In a large bowl, whisk together flour, sugar, cocoa, baking soda, and salt. In a separate bowl, whisk together coffee, oil, vinegar, and vanilla. Pour the wet mixture into the dry mixture and whisk until just combined. Do not overmix. Fold in crushed cookie pieces.

Fill the cupcake liners about two-thirds full with batter. Bake for 16 to 20 minutes, or until a toothpick inserted in the center of the cupcake comes out dry with a few crumbs clinging to it. Let the cupcakes cool completely before frosting.

To make the frosting: Using a stand or hand mixer, beat shortening until smooth. With the mixer running on low, add powdered sugar, peppermint extract, and 1 tablespoon nondairy milk at a time, as needed, until frosting reaches a spreadable consistency. Increase the speed to high and beat for 2 more minutes until light and fluffy. Add crushed cookie pieces and beat until incorporated. Add more nondairy milk, if needed.

To assemble the cupcakes: Spread a layer of frosting on the cupcakes. Garnish each cupcake with a mint leaf and half a cookie.

Maple-Glazed Carrot Cupcakes

MAKES 18 CUPCAKES

These moist and perfectly spiced carrot cupcakes are so delicious in their simplicity that I like to top them with nothing more than a light coating of maple glaze.

Make-Ahead Tip:
Cupcakes can be made in advance and frozen, unfrosted, for up to 1 month. Thaw cupcakes and glaze before serving.

CUPCAKES

2 cups all-purpose flour*	½ cup canola oil
1 cup sugar	1 tablespoon white or apple-cider
1 teaspoon baking powder	vinegar
½ teaspoon baking soda	1 tablespoon pure vanilla extract
1 teaspoon salt	2 cups peeled, grated carrots
1 teaspoon ground cinnamon	(about 3 large carrots)
½ teaspoon ground nutmeg	1 cup raisins
1 cup carrot or orange juice	

GLAZE

1½ cups powdered sugar	1 to 3 tablespoons water
3 tablespoons maple syrup	

To make the cupcakes: Preheat the oven to 350 degrees. Line two 12-cup cupcake pans with 16 cupcake liners.

In a large bowl, whisk together flour, sugar, baking powder, baking soda, salt, cinnamon, and nutmeg. In a separate bowl, whisk together carrot or orange juice, oil, vinegar, and vanilla. Pour the wet mixture into the dry mixture and whisk until just combined. Do not overmix. Gently fold in carrots and raisins (see Tip, page 122).

*For a gluten-free alternative, substitute gluten-free all-purpose flour plus 1 teaspoon xanthan gum and see page 11.

Fill the cupcake liners about two-thirds full with batter. Bake for about 20 minutes, or until a toothpick inserted in the center of the cupcake comes out dry with a few crumbs clinging to it. Let the cupcakes cool completely before frosting.

To make the glaze: In a medium bowl, whisk together powdered sugar, maple syrup, and 1 tablespoon water at a time, until smooth.

To assemble the cupcakes: Drizzle the glaze over the cupcakes. Let set and serve.

Coffee Almond Crunch Cupcakes

Want to prove to someone that you're a cupcake rock star? This is your cupcake! They are the ultimate, decadent, melt-in-your-mouth masterpieces. If you want to impress, make these cupcakes!

Make-Ahead Tip:

Cupcakes can be made in advance and frozen, unfrosted, for up to 1 month. Frosting can be made the day before and stored at room temperature. Thaw cupcakes and assemble before serving.

CUPCAKES

1½ cups all-purpose flour*	1 cup canned coconut milk,
1 cup sugar	mixed well before measuring
⅓ cup unsweetened cocoa powder	½ cup canola oil
1 teaspoon baking soda	2 tablespoons white or apple-cider
½ teaspoon salt	vinegar
	1 tablespoon pure vanilla extract
	2 teaspoons instant espresso powder

FROSTING

1 cup non-hydrogenated vegetable	3 tablespoons instant espresso
shortening	powder dissolved in ¼ cup
3 cups powdered sugar	water
1 teaspoon pure vanilla extract	

GANACHE

1 cup semisweet chocolate chips	¼ cup canned coconut milk,
(dairy-free)	mixed well before measuring
	2 tablespoons canola oil
1 cup chopped toasted almonds	Chocolate-covered espresso beans,
	for garnish

*For a gluten-free alternative, substitute gluten-free all-purpose flour plus ¾ teaspoon xanthan gum and see page 11.

To make the cupcakes: Preheat the oven to 350 degrees. Line two 12-cup cupcake pans with 14 cupcake liners.

In a large bowl, whisk together flour, sugar, cocoa, baking soda, and salt. In a separate bowl, whisk together coconut milk, oil, vinegar, vanilla, and espresso powder. Pour the wet mixture into the dry mixture and whisk until just combined. Do not overmix.

Fill the cupcake liners about two-thirds full with batter. Bake for 16 to 20 minutes, or until a toothpick inserted in the center of the cupcake comes out dry with a few crumbs clinging to it. Cool the cupcakes completely before frosting.

To make the frosting: Using a stand or hand mixer, beat shortening until smooth. With the mixer running on low, add powdered sugar and vanilla, and beat to incorporate. Add 1 tablespoon of espresso liquid at a time, as needed, until it reaches desired frosting consistency and espresso flavor. Increase speed to high and beat for 2 more minutes until light and fluffy.

To make the ganache: Melt chocolate chips and coconut milk in a double boiler or microwave. Whisk in oil until smooth.

To assemble the cupcakes: Once the cupcakes are completely cooled, slice the dome off the top of each cupcake and pipe with a layer of frosting. Place the top of the cupcake back on top of the frosting. Spread a thin layer of ganache over the dome of the cupcake and sprinkle with almonds. Garnish with an additional bit of frosting and espresso bean.

Pumpkin Whoopie Pies

MAKES ABOUT 16 WHOOPIE PIES

Your friends will be screaming "Whoopie!" when you set a tray of these whoopie pies on the table. I make them year 'round using canned pumpkin because they are too delicious to save for autumn.

Make-Ahead Tip:

Whoopies can be made in advance and frozen, unfrosted, for up to 1 month. Filling can be made the day before and stored at room temperature. Thaw whoopies and assemble before serving.

PIES

2 cups all-purpose flour*
1 cup sugar
1 teaspoon baking powder
½ teaspoon baking soda
1 teaspoon salt
1 teaspoon ground ginger
1 teaspoon ground nutmeg
½ teaspoon ground cloves
½ teaspoon ground cinnamon

1 cup pumpkin puree, canned or
   cooked fresh
1 cup canned coconut milk,
   mixed well before measuring
½ cup canola oil
1 tablespoon white or apple-cider
   vinegar
1 tablespoon pure vanilla extract

BUTTERCREAM

1 cup non-hydrogenated vegetable
   shortening
3 cups powdered sugar
2 tablespoons pure maple syrup

2 teaspoons pure vanilla extract
1 to 3 tablespoons soy, almond,
   or rice milk

Powdered sugar, for serving

To make the pies: Preheat the oven to 350 degrees. Lightly grease a whoopie pie pan or line a large baking sheet with parchment paper.

*For a gluten-free alternative, substitute gluten-free all-purpose flour plus 1 teaspoon xanthan gum and see page 11.

In a large bowl, whisk together flour, sugar, baking powder, baking soda, salt, ginger, nutmeg, cloves, and cinnamon. In a separate bowl, whisk together pumpkin puree, coconut milk, oil, vinegar, and vanilla. Pour the wet mixture into the dry mixture and whisk until just combined. Do not overmix.

Scoop about 2 to 3 tablespoons of batter into each cup of the whoopie pie pan or onto the prepared baking sheet, leaving about 4 inches between each whoopie. Bake for 10 to 12 minutes, or until a toothpick inserted in the center of the whoopie comes out clean. Let the whoopies cool completely in the pan before unmolding.

To make the buttercream: Using a stand or hand mixer, beat the shortening until smooth. With the mixer running on low, add powdered sugar, maple syrup, vanilla extract, and 1 tablespoon nondairy milk at a time, as needed, until frosting reaches a spreadable consistency. Increase speed to high and beat for 2 more minutes until light and fluffy.

To assemble the pies: Spread a layer of the buttercream on the flat bottom side of 16 pies and sandwich with the remaining pies. Dust with powdered sugar before serving.

Bollywood Cupcakes

MAKES 12 CUPCAKES

One of my best friends from college, Niki, is a professional Bollywood dancer and choreographer. So cool, right? I minored in modern dance, but Niki taught me how to turn up the funk and move to those fast Bollywood beats! Sometimes we performed together, and I would always bring these Indian-inspired cupcakes to rehearsal. Traditional Indian spices like saffron and cardamom work beautifully in a cupcake.

Make-Ahead Tip:

Cupcakes can be made in advance and frozen, unfrosted, for up to 1 month. Frosting can be made the day before and stored at room temperature. Thaw cupcakes and frost before serving.

CUPCAKES

¾ cup soy, almond, or rice milk

½ teaspoon saffron threads

1½ cups all-purpose flour*

1 cup sugar

1 teaspoon baking soda

½ teaspoon salt

⅓ cup canola oil

2 tablespoons white or apple cider vinegar

1 tablespoon pure vanilla extract

BUTTERCREAM

1 cup non-hydrogenated vegetable shortening

3 cups powdered sugar

1 teaspoon pure vanilla extract

1 tablespoon ground cardamom

3 to 5 tablespoons soy, almond, or rice milk

Gold pearls or dust for garnish, optional

To make the cupcakes: Preheat the oven to 350 degrees. Line a 12-cup cupcake pan with cupcake liners and spray with nonstick cooking oil.

In a small saucepan, combine nondairy milk and saffron. Bring to a boil, then remove from heat and let cool.

*For a gluten-free alternative, substitute gluten-free all-purpose flour plus ¾ teaspoon xanthan gum and see page 11.

In a large bowl, whisk together flour, sugar, baking soda, and salt. In a separate bowl, whisk together cooled saffron mixture, oil, vinegar, and vanilla. Pour the wet mixture into the dry mixture and whisk until just combined. Do not overmix.

Fill the cupcake liners about two-thirds full with batter. Bake for about 20 minutes, or until a toothpick inserted in the center of the cupcake comes out dry with a few crumbs clinging to it. Let the cupcakes cool completely before frosting.

To make the buttercream: Using a stand or hand mixer, beat the shortening until smooth. With the mixer running on low, add powdered sugar, vanilla, cardamom, and 1 tablespoon nondairy milk at a time, as needed, until frosting reaches a spreadable consistency. Increase speed to high and beat for 2 more minutes until light and fluffy.

To assemble the cupcakes: Pipe or spread a thin layer of buttercream on the cupcakes. If desired, garnish with gold pearls or dust.

Cinnamon Mocha Cupcakes

MAKES 14 CUPCAKES

Most college students are addicted to coffee, but my friends in college were addicted to Cinnamon Mocha Cupcakes. They would request them for every study session, which meant I was pulling batches out of the oven nearly every week. My sweet roommate, Cindy, always loved to help—so you can guess how we liked to spend our time together during finals week!

Make-Ahead Tip:

Cupcakes can be made in advance and frozen, unfrosted, for up to 1 month. Frosting can be made the day before and stored at room temperature. Thaw cupcakes and frost before serving.

CUPCAKES

1½ cups all-purpose flour*

1 cup sugar

¼ cup unsweetened cocoa powder

1 teaspoon baking soda

1 teaspoon ground cinnamon

½ teaspoon salt

1 cup canned coconut milk, mixed well before measuring

½ cup canola oil

2 tablespoons white or apple-cider vinegar

1 tablespoon pure vanilla extract

2 teaspoons instant espresso powder

FROSTING

1 cup non-hydrogenated vegetable shortening

3 cups powdered sugar

1 teaspoon pure vanilla extract

2 tablespoons instant espresso powder dissolved in ¼ cup water

Ground cinnamon, for serving

Chocolate curls, for garnish (see Tip, page 177)

To make the cupcakes: Preheat the oven to 350 degrees. Line two 12-cup cupcake pans with 14 cupcake liners.

*For a gluten-free alternative, substitute gluten-free all-purpose flour plus ¾ teaspoon xanthan gum and see page 11.

In a large bowl, whisk together flour, sugar, cocoa, baking soda, cinnamon, and salt. In a separate bowl, whisk together coconut milk, oil, vinegar, vanilla, and espresso powder. Pour the wet mixture into the dry mixture and whisk until just combined. Do not overmix.

Fill the cupcake liners about two-thirds full with batter. Bake for 16 to 20 minutes, or until a toothpick inserted in the center of the cupcake comes out dry with a few crumbs clinging to it. Let the cupcakes cool completely before frosting.

To make the frosting: Using a stand or hand mixer, beat shortening until smooth. With the mixer running on low, add powdered sugar and vanilla, and beat to incorporate. Add 1 tablespoon of espresso liquid at a time, as needed, until it reaches desired frosting consistency and espresso flavor. Increase speed to high and beat for 2 more minutes until light and fluffy.

To assemble the cupcakes: Pipe or spread a layer of frosting on the cupcakes. Dust with cinnamon and garnish with chocolate curls.

Chloe's Tip: Making Chocolate Curls

To make chocolate curls, run a vegetable peeler along one edge of a bar of chocolate. If the chocolate breaks into small pieces, the chocolate is too hard. Microwave the chocolate for about 10 seconds to get it soft enough to form curls. Place the curls on a plate and refrigerate immediately, so that they don't get crushed. Use a toothpick to hook and pick up the curls and place them on your dessert.

Chocolate Beer Cupcakes
with Irish Whiskey Buttercream

MAKES 14 CUPCAKES

These moist, chocolaty cupcakes are laced with a rich stout flavor, topped with a sweet 'n' boozy buttercream, and drizzled with a fig caramel. If only they sold these at my local pub, I'd be a regular!

Make-Ahead Tip:

Cupcakes can be made in advance and frozen, unfrosted, for up to 1 month. Frosting can be made the day before and stored at room temperature. Thaw cupcakes and assemble before serving.

CUPCAKES

1½ cups all-purpose flour*	½ cup canola oil
1 cup sugar	2 tablespoons white or apple-cider vinegar
⅓ cup unsweetened cocoa powder	
1 teaspoon baking soda	1 tablespoon pure vanilla extract
½ teaspoon salt	
1 cup stout beer	

BUTTERCREAM

1 cup non-hydrogenated vegetable shortening	2 to 5 tablespoons soy, almond, or rice milk
3 cups powdered sugar	3 to 4 teaspoons Irish whiskey
1 teaspoon pure vanilla extract	

FIG CARAMEL

6 dried figs, stems removed	2 tablespoons water
½ cup pure maple syrup	¼ teaspoon ground cinnamon

To make the cupcakes: Preheat the oven to 350 degrees. Line two 12-cup cupcake pans with 14 cupcake liners.

*For a gluten-free alternative, substitute gluten-free all-purpose flour plus ¾ teaspoon xanthan gum and see page 11.

In a large bowl, whisk together flour, sugar, cocoa, baking soda, and salt. In a separate bowl, whisk together beer, oil, vinegar, and vanilla. Pour the wet mixture into the dry mixture and whisk until just combined. Do not overmix.

Fill the cupcake liners about two-thirds full with batter. Bake for 18 to 22 minutes, or until a toothpick inserted in the center of the cupcake comes out dry with a few crumbs clinging to it. Let the cupcakes cool completely before frosting.

To make the buttercream: Using a stand or hand mixer, beat shortening until smooth. With the mixer running on low, add powdered sugar, vanilla, and 1 tablespoon nondairy milk at a time, as needed, until frosting reaches a spreadable consistency. Add whiskey, 1 teaspoon at a time, until desired whiskey flavor is reached. Increase the speed to high and beat for 2 more minutes until light and fluffy.

To make the fig caramel: Place figs in a small saucepan with water to cover and bring to a gentle boil. Let the dates boil gently for 10 minutes. Drain and rinse with cold water until cool to the touch. Coarsely chop the figs. Place in a blender; add maple syrup, water, and cinnamon. Blend until smooth. Store in the refrigerator until ready to use.

To assemble the cupcakes: Pipe or spread a layer of buttercream on the cupcakes. Dust with cocoa powder. Drizzle the fig caramel over the cupcakes using a spoon or squeeze bottle.

Raspberry Chocolate Mousse Cupcakes

These rich chocolate cupcakes filled with a raspberry reduction and topped with velvety mousse will prove to even the most stubborn cupcake connoisseur that vegan cupcakes rock! They also make the perfect Valentine's Day dessert.

Note: The Chocolate Mousse will need to chill in the refrigerator for 8 hours or overnight before assembly.

Make-Ahead Tip:

Cupcakes can be made in advance and frozen, unfrosted, for up to 1 month. Raspberry filling can be stored in the refrigerator for up to 1 week. Thaw cupcakes and frost before serving.

MOUSSE

¼ cup soy, almond, or rice milk

1 teaspoon instant espresso powder, optional

1 cup semisweet chocolate chips (dairy-free)

1 (13.5-ounce) can of coconut milk (not lite), preferably Thai Kitchen brand or Whole Foods 365 brand, chilled, not stirred

½ cup powdered sugar

FILLING

1 (12-ounce) bag frozen raspberries or 2 cups fresh raspberries

2 tablespoons water

¼ cup sugar

⅛ teaspoon salt

1 teaspoon lemon juice

CUPCAKES

1½ cups all-purpose flour*

1 cup sugar

⅓ cup unsweetened cocoa powder

1 teaspoon baking soda

½ teaspoon salt

1 cup cold coffee or water

½ cup canola oil

2 tablespoons white or apple-cider vinegar

1 tablespoon pure vanilla extract

*For a gluten-free alternative, substitute gluten-free all-purpose flour plus ¾ teaspoon xanthan gum and see page 11.

To make the mousse: Chill the bowl and whisk of a stand mixer in the freezer for about 10 minutes. In the meantime, whisk nondairy milk and espresso powder in a medium sauce-pan over medium heat. Once the espresso powder is incorporated, add chocolate chips and whisk over low heat until the chocolate is melted and smooth. Pour the mixture into a large bowl, let cool, and then chill in the refrigerator until cool to the touch, about 15 minutes. The chocolate should still be soft and pliable; if it has chilled and hardened, let it sit at room temperature for a few minutes until softened.

Skim the solidified coconut cream from the chilled can of coconut milk and transfer the solids to the bowl of the stand mixer. Do not include any of the coconut water, even if you have to leave behind a little margin of coconut cream (even a little bit of coconut water can harm your results).

Add powdered sugar and beat for 1 to 2 minutes until fluffy. Add the cooled chocolate mix-ture to the stand mixer and beat until incorporated. Let chill, covered, in the refrigerator for 8 hours or overnight.

To make the filling: In a medium saucepan, cook raspberries, water, sugar, and salt over medium heat for about 15 minutes, or until thick and saucy. Remove from heat and stir in lemon juice. Let cool, then store in the refrigerator.

To make the cupcakes: Preheat the oven to 350 degrees. Line two 12-cup cupcake pans with 14 cupcake liners.

In a large bowl, whisk together flour, sugar, cocoa, baking soda, and salt. In a separate bowl, whisk together coffee, oil, vinegar, and vanilla. Pour the wet mixture into the dry mixture and whisk until just combined. Do not overmix.

Fill the cupcake liners about two-thirds full with batter. Bake for 16 to 20 minutes, or until a toothpick inserted in the center of the cupcake comes out dry with a few crumbs clinging to it. Let the cupcakes cool completely before frosting.

To assemble the cupcakes: Using a knife or spoon, gently cut out a couple teaspoons of cake from the top of the cupcake and discard (or eat!), to create a small hole. Fill the hole with a couple teaspoons of filling and top with mousse.

PUPcakes

Let them eat cake! The dogs, that is. Why should they be left out of the cupcake craze? My two newly adopted Chihuahuas, Winnie and Buster, enjoyed these on their first birthday. PUPcakes also make a great gift for fellow dog lovers.

Make-Ahead Tip:
PUPcakes can be made in advance and frozen, for up to 2 months. Thaw before serving.

1 cup whole-wheat flour
1 teaspoon baking soda
½ cup unsweetened applesauce
¼ cup canola oil

¼ cup water
1 tablespoon apple-cider vinegar
¾ cup vegan carob chips

Preheat the oven to 350 degrees. Generously grease a mini cupcake pan.

In a large bowl, whisk together flour and baking soda. In a separate bowl, whisk together applesauce, oil, water, and vinegar. Pour the wet mixture into the dry mixture and whisk until just combined. Do not overmix.

Fill each cup about two-thirds full with batter. Bake for 10 to 12 minutes, or until a tooth-pick inserted in the center of the cupcake comes out dry. Let the cupcakes cool completely, then run a knife around the rim of each cupcake cup and gently unmold.

Melt carob chips in a double boiler or microwave (see Tip, page 185). Whisk until smooth and spread a thin layer on each cupcake. Let set and serve to the pups. Depending on the size of your dog, you may want to cut the cupcake in half or quarters.

Chloe's Tip: Melting Carob

Carob melts much faster than chocolate because of its low fat content. If using a microwave, set the power to medium and check every 10 seconds. If using a double boiler, heat over medium/low and check often. You can also add a teaspoon of canola oil to the carob before melting it for an extra-smooth and shiny look.

Agave-Sweetened Chocolate Cake

MAKES ONE 9-INCH ROUND LAYER.
DOUBLE THE RECIPE FOR TWO LAYERS.

Use this recipe as a refined sugar-free alternative to chocolate cake. Top it with your favorite frosting, or, to make an entirely refined-sugar-free dessert, drizzle it with Crème Anglaise (page 236) and fresh berries. This batter will also make about 17 cupcakes, baked for 16 to 18 minutes.

1½ cups all-purpose flour*
⅓ cup unsweetened cocoa powder
1 teaspoon baking soda
½ teaspoon salt
1 cup agave

¾ cup soy, almond, or rice milk
½ cup canola oil
2 tablespoons white or apple-cider vinegar
2 teaspoons pure vanilla extract

Preheat the oven to 350 degrees. Lightly grease a 9-inch round cake pan and line the bottom with parchment paper.

In a large bowl, whisk together flour, cocoa, baking soda, and salt. In a separate bowl, whisk together agave, nondairy milk, oil, vinegar, and vanilla. Pour the wet mixture into the dry mixture and whisk until just combined. Do not overmix.

Fill the prepared cake pan evenly with batter. Bake for 30 to 35 minutes, or until a toothpick inserted in the center of the cake comes out dry with a few crumbs clinging to it. Rotate the cake halfway through baking time. Let the cake cool completely before unmolding.

*For a gluten-free alternative, substitute gluten-free all-purpose flour plus ¾ teaspoon xanthan gum and see page 11.

Chloe's Vegan Desserts

Agave-Sweetened Vanilla Cake

MAKES ONE 9-INCH ROUND LAYER.
DOUBLE THE RECIPE FOR TWO LAYERS.

Use this recipe as a refined sugar-free alternative to vanilla cake. Top it with your favorite frosting or, to make an entirely refined-sugar-free dessert, drizzle it with Crème Anglaise (page 236) and fresh berries. This batter will also make about 17 cupcakes, baked for 14 to 16 minutes.

1¾ cups all-purpose flour*	¾ cup agave
1 teaspoon baking soda	½ cup canola oil
1 teaspoon baking powder	1 tablespoon white or apple-cider
½ teaspoon salt	vinegar
1 cup soy, almond, or rice milk	2 teaspoons pure vanilla extract

Preheat the oven to 350 degrees. Lightly grease a 9-inch round cake pan and line the bottom with parchment paper.

In a large bowl, whisk together flour, baking soda, baking powder, and salt. In a separate bowl, whisk together nondairy milk, agave, oil, vinegar, and vanilla. Pour the wet mixture into the dry mixture and whisk until just combined. Do not overmix. Batter will be thin.

Fill the prepared cake pan evenly with batter. Bake for about 30 minutes, or until a toothpick inserted in the center of the cake comes out dry with a few crumbs clinging to it. Rotate the cake halfway through baking time. Let the cake cool completely before unmolding.

*For a gluten-free alternative, substitute gluten-free all-purpose flour plus ¾ teaspoon xanthan gum and see page 11.

Spoon
Desserts

Praline Pecan Ice Cream

MAKES 1 QUART

Praline pecan was one of my favorite ice cream flavors as a child, so when I went vegan, I had no choice but to invent this dairy-free recipe. I used it as my secret weapon on multiple culinary school exams, leaving my teachers thoroughly amazed! I highly suggest you add this one to your ice cream repertoire.

1 quart store-bought Vanilla Ice Cream (dairy-free) (page 237), or use store-bought
1 cup brown sugar
¼ cup vegan margarine

2 tablespoons soy, almond, or rice milk
1½ cups pecans, toasted and chopped

Soften ice cream in the refrigerator for about 15 to 30 minutes, unless using freshly made ice cream.

In a small saucepan over medium heat, heat brown sugar, margarine, and nondairy milk, stirring frequently. Once the mixture comes together, increase heat to medium-high for 1 minute. Remove from heat, stir in pecans, and let sit 15 to 20 minutes, stirring occasionally.

Transfer ice cream to a large bowl and fold in as much of the pecan mixture as you would like. Reserve any remaining pecan mixture for another use. Cover bowl tightly with plastic wrap, making sure that the plastic wrap is pressed onto the top of the ice cream.

Rosemary Ice Cream with Blueberry Sauce

MAKES 1 QUART

I know it sounds strange, but trust me that this flavor combo is a winner. The fresh herb-infused ice cream has a sweet and subtle flavor that is complimented perfectly by the vibrant Blueberry Sauce. Even kids will enjoy this seemingly daring dessert.

ICE CREAM

1 (13.5-ounce) can coconut milk	3 tablespoons canola oil
1½ cups almond or soy milk	½ teaspoon pure vanilla extract
3 sprigs fresh rosemary	⅛ teaspoon salt
¾ cup agave	¾ teaspoon xanthan or guar gum

SAUCE

1 (12-ounce) bag frozen blueberries or 2 cups fresh	¼ cup sugar
	1 teaspoon lemon juice
2 tablespoons water	⅛ teaspoon salt

To make the ice cream: In a small saucepan, combine coconut milk and almond or soy milk. Bring to a simmer and add rosemary. Reduce heat to low, and let cook, covered, for 20 minutes, stirring occasionally. Remove rosemary and let cool completely.

Blend rosemary-infused milk, agave, oil, vanilla, salt, and xanthan gum in a blender until thoroughly combined. Chill in the refrigerator for 2 to 3 hours. Once the ice cream base is chilled, pour it into an ice cream maker and process according to manufacturer's instructions.

To make the sauce: In a medium saucepan, cook blueberries, water, and sugar over medium heat for about 15 minutes, or until thick and saucy. Remove from heat and stir in lemon juice and salt. Add the sauce to a blender, and blend until smooth. For a smoother sauce, press through a fine-mesh strainer to remove the pulp. Let cool, then store in refrigerator.

To serve: If the ice cream is too hard to scoop, let it soften in the refrigerator for 15 to 30 minutes. Top each scoop of rosemary ice cream with a spoonful of blueberry sauce and serve immediately.

Chocolate Hazelnut Gelato

MAKES 1 QUART

Adding a tablespoon of hazelnut liqueur is the secret ingredient in this ultra-creamy gelato. Alcohol lowers the freezing point of liquids; so adding a splash of alcohol to your ice cream base prevents ice crystals and ensures a smooth, creamy texture.

1 (13.5-ounce) can coconut milk
2 cups almond or soy milk
¾ cup agave
⅛ teaspoon salt
¾ teaspoon xanthan or guar gum

½ cup unsweetened cocoa powder
3 tablespoons hazelnut butter
1 tablespoon Frangelico or other
　hazelnut liqueur

Blend coconut milk, almond milk, agave, salt, xanthan gum, cocoa, hazelnut butter, and liqueur in a blender. Chill in the refrigerator for 2 to 3 hours. Once the ice cream base is chilled, pour it into an ice cream maker and process following manufacturer's instructions.

Coconut Sorbet with Cashew Brittle

SERVES 4

This island dessert is refreshing and easy to whip up. I always keep a bag of cashew brittle in my freezer for those days when I'm craving a sweet crunch. I love it on coconut sorbet, but you could add it to any sorbet or ice cream flavor you'd like.

1 cup sugar

¼ cup water

1 cup cashews

1 pint coconut sorbet

Line a large baking sheet with parchment paper or Silpat. In a medium saucepan, combine sugar and water. Bring to a gentle boil over medium-high heat and let cook for about 8 to 12 minutes until golden, whisking occasionally. Add cashews and remove from heat. Pour mixture onto the prepared baking sheet and let cool completely.

Once cooled and hardened, transfer to a cutting board and roughly chop into clusters with a sharp knife. Store in freezer.

To serve, top a scoop of coconut sorbet with a spoonful of cashew brittle.

Chocolate Mousse

SERVES 10

Calling all chocolate lovers! Try this velvet chocolate mousse recipe that is extremely easy and melt-in-your-mouth delicious. The mousse has a light fluffy texture and rich chocolate flavor. The best part? It is served in an elegant chocolate cup so you can have your dessert cup and eat it too!

Note: The Chocolate Mousse will need to chill in the refrigerator for 8 hours or overnight before serving.

Cups

1 cup semisweet chocolate chips
    (dairy-free)

MOUSSE

½ cup soy, almond, or rice milk

1 teaspoon instant espresso powder,
    optional

1 cup semisweet chocolate chips
    (dairy-free)

1 (13.5-ounce) can of coconut
    milk (not lite), preferably
    Thai Kitchen brand or
    Whole Foods 365 brand,
    chilled, not stirred

⅓ cup powdered sugar

Raspberry Sauce (page 233), optional

To make the cups: Melt chocolate chips over a double boiler until smooth. Line a 12-cup cupcake tray with 10 paper liners and pour approximately 1 tablespoon melted chocolate into each cup. Use a pastry brush to evenly coat each cupcake liner and spread the chocolate up the sides of each liner, stopping about ½ inch from the top. Freeze tray for several hours or overnight. Peel off the cupcake wrappers and . . . ta-da! Edible chocolate cups! Store in freezer.

To make the mousse: Chill the bowl and whisk of a stand mixer in the freezer for about 10 minutes. In the meantime, whisk nondairy milk and espresso powder in a medium saucepan over medium heat. Once espresso is incorporated, add chocolate chips and whisk over low heat until the chocolate is melted and smooth. Pour the mixture into a large bowl, let cool, then chill in the refrigerator until cool to the touch, about 15 minutes. The chocolate should still be soft and pliable; if it has chilled and hardened, let it sit at room temperature for a few minutes until softened.

Skim the solidified coconut cream from the chilled coconut milk and transfer the solids to the bowl of the stand mixer. Do not include any of the coconut water, even if you have to leave behind a little margin of coconut cream (even a little bit of coconut water can harm your results).

Add powdered sugar and beat for 1 to 2 minutes, until fluffy. Add the cooled chocolate mixture and beat until incorporated. Let chill, covered, in the refrigerator for 8 hours or overnight. Distribute evenly among 10 chocolate cups. Each serving will be a little about ¼ cup of mousse. Drizzle with Raspberry Sauce, if using.

Chloe's Vegan Desserts

Classic Crème Brûlée

SERVES 4

Turn your kitchen into a fancy French restaurant by whipping up this dessert! Traditionally, crème brûlée is loaded with eggs and dairy, but my vegan version is easy, light, and delicious. If you don't have crème brûlée dishes, try making this in ramekins or coffee mugs.

Note: The custard will need to chill in the refrigerator for 8 hours or overnight before torching.

¼ cup soy, almond, or rice milk
¼ cup cornstarch or arrowroot
1 (13.5-ounce) can coconut milk
½ cup sugar, plus extra for brûlée
⅛ teaspoon salt

Seeds scraped from 1 vanilla bean or 1 teaspoon pure vanilla extract
1 drop natural yellow food coloring, optional

In a small bowl, thoroughly mix nondairy milk and cornstarch with a whisk or fork and set aside.

In a medium saucepan, whisk together coconut milk, ½ cup sugar, and salt, and heat over medium-high heat just until boiling. Reduce the heat to medium and slowly drizzle the cornstarch mixture into the saucepan, whisking continuously. Let cook until the mixture becomes very thick in texture, like pudding, about 5 minutes, whisking frequently. Remove from heat and whisk in vanilla and food coloring, if using.

Pour the custard evenly into 4 crème brûlée dishes or ramekins. Smooth tops. Let cool for 10 minutes; then chill in the refrigerator for 8 hours or overnight.

Remove the custards from the refrigerator 1 hour before torching, so that they come to room temperature. Sprinkle about 2 teaspoons sugar onto each custard, then give it a little shake so that the sugar spreads evenly.

Hold a torch about 2 to 3 inches from the sugar and melt the sugar until it bubbles and turns slightly golden. Be sure to move your torch back and forth continuously so that it does not burn in one spot. Once there is no more visible dry sugar, let the crème brûlée sit for 3 to 5 minutes, then serve immediately.

Note: For an extra-thick crackly top, add 2 more teaspoons of sugar and repeat the torching process.

Sticky Toffee Pudding

MAKES 14 PUDDING CAKES

Hear ye, hear ye! Behold the vegan version of England's iconic dessert. Sticky Toffee Pudding is the favorite dessert of Catherine, Duchess of Cambridge (better known as Kate Middleton), and I must say that I am not surprised. With a sweet moist date cake that is smothered in sticky toffee glaze, this creation is truly fit for royalty.

GLAZE

1 cup canned coconut milk, mixed well before measuring	4 tablespoons vegan margarine
1 cup dark brown sugar	¼ teaspoon salt

PUDDING CAKES

16 (about 8 ounces) Medjool dates, pitted	½ teaspoon salt
1 cup canned coconut milk, mixed well before measuring	½ teaspoon ground cinnamon
	1 cup brown sugar
2 cups all-purpose flour*	½ cup canola oil
½ teaspoon baking soda	2 teaspoons white or apple cider vinegar
1 teaspoon baking powder	1 tablespoon pure vanilla extract

To make the glaze: In a medium saucepan, combine coconut milk, brown sugar, margarine, and salt. Bring to a boil over medium-high heat, stirring occasionally. Let cook for about 5 minutes and remove from heat.

To make the cakes: Preheat the oven to 350 degrees. Lightly grease two 12-cup cupcake pans. Prepare a grid cooling rack by fitting it on top of a large baking sheet.

Place dates in a small saucepan with water to cover, and bring to a gentle boil. Let the dates boil gently for 10 minutes. Drain and place in a food processor or blender with coconut milk. Process until combined and set aside.

*For a gluten-free alternative, substitute gluten-free all-purpose flour plus 1 teaspoon xanthan gum and see page 11.

In a large bowl, whisk flour, baking soda, baking powder, salt, and cinnamon. In the bowl of a stand mixer, beat the date mixture, brown sugar, oil, vinegar, and vanilla. Slowly add the flour mixture and beat until just combined.

Fill the cupcake cups about two-thirds full with batter. Bake for 18 to 20 minutes, or until a toothpick inserted in the center of the cake comes out clean with a few crumbs clinging to it. Remove from oven and, using a toothpick, immediately tilt the cakes so that they sit in the cupcake pans at an angle. Pour 2 tablespoons of glaze into each cupcake cup, then nudge the cakes so that they sit back into the cups. Let soak for about 10 minutes, then flip onto the prepared cooling rack. Top each cake with an extra tablespoon of glaze and serve immediately.

Rum Raisin Rice Pudding

SERVES 10

Sweet 'n' creamy rice pudding dotted with boozy raisins—spoon-fed perfection! For a fancy presentation, serve it in a cocktail glass. Technically, this dessert should be fully chilled before serving but, if you're like me, you might sneak a taste of it while it's warm. If you're making this for kids, omit the rum.

Note: The pudding will need to chill in the refrigerator for 8 hours or overnight before serving.

¾ cup raisins

3 tablespoons dark rum

1 cup uncooked Arborio or other medium-grain white rice

5 cups soy, almond, or rice milk

½ cup sugar

½ teaspoon salt

¼ teaspoon ground cinnamon

1 teaspoon pure vanilla extract

In a small bowl, soak raisins in rum and set aside.

In a large pot, combine rice, nondairy milk, sugar, salt, and cinnamon. Bring to a boil over medium-high heat, then reduce heat to low. Simmer, uncovered, stirring occasionally, for 45 to 50 minutes until thickened. Transfer to a large bowl and stir in vanilla, raisins, and rum. Let cool completely, cover with plastic wrap, and chill in the refrigerator for 8 hours or overnight.

Pistachio Pots de Crème

SERVES 4

Pots de crème (pronounced Poh-da-KREM) is French custard, looser in texture than other custards and puddings. Using homemade pistachio milk instead of cream creates the same smooth texture and adds a nice nutty flavor.

Note: The pots de crème will need to chill in the refrigerator for 8 hours or overnight before serving.

1¼ cups water, divided
3 tablespoons cornstarch or arrowroot
½ cup shelled unsalted pistachios*
½ cup sugar

⅛ teaspoon salt
¼ cup semisweet chocolate chips
   (dairy-free)

In a small bowl, thoroughly mix ¼ cup water and cornstarch with a whisk or fork and set aside.

In a blender, make pistachio milk by combining remaining 1 cup water and pistachios. Blend on high for 2 minutes until completely smooth. In a medium saucepan, whisk together pistachio milk, sugar, and salt, and heat on medium-high just until boiling. Reduce the heat to low, and stir in chocolate chips. Let cook, whisking frequently, until completely smooth. Increase the heat to medium and slowly drizzle the cornstarch mixture into the saucepan, whisking continuously. Let cook until the mixture becomes very thick in texture, like pudding, about 5 minutes, whisking frequently.

Pour the custard evenly into 4 ramekins or small cups. Smooth the tops. Let cool for 10 minutes, then chill in the refrigerator for 8 hours or overnight.

*If you are not using a high-powered blender, such as a Vitamix, soak overnight or boil for 10 minutes and drain. This will soften the pistachios and ensure a silky smooth cream.

Panna Cotta

SERVES 4

Traditional Italian panna cotta is made with gelatin, but using cornstarch or arrowroot keeps it vegan, yet gives it the same gelatinous texture. Serve it with Raspberry Sauce (page 233) or Chocolate Sauce (page 232) and any other toppings you would like.

Note: The Panna Cotta will need to chill in the refrigerator for 8 hours or overnight before unmolding.

¼ cup soy, almond, or rice milk
¼ cup cornstarch or arrowroot
1 (13.5-ounce) can coconut milk
½ cup sugar

⅛ teaspoon salt
Seeds scraped from 1 vanilla bean
    or 1 teaspoon pure vanilla
    extract

Raspberry Sauce (page 233), optional

Chocolate Sauce (page 232), optional

In a small bowl, thoroughly mix nondairy milk and cornstarch with a whisk or fork and set aside.

In a medium saucepan, whisk coconut milk, sugar, and salt, and heat over medium-high just until boiling. Reduce heat to medium and slowly drizzle the cornstarch mixture into the saucepan, whisking continuously. Let cook until the mixture becomes very thick in texture, like pudding, about 5 minutes, whisking frequently. Remove from heat and whisk in vanilla.

Pour the custard evenly into 4 ramekins. Smooth the tops. Let cool for 10 minutes; then chill in the refrigerator for 8 hours or overnight.

Remove the custards from the refrigerator 1 hour before torching, so that they come to room temperature. Sprinkle about 2 teaspoons sugar onto each custard, then give it a little shake so that the sugar spreads evenly.

Gently shake each ramekin to loosen edges. Place a plate on top of each ramekin and flip with force to unmold. Garnish with Raspberry Sauce (see Tip, page 211), if desired.

Chloe's Tip: Decorating the Plate

If you want to drizzle your raspberry sauce in a way that is elegant and simple, try using a squeeze bottle to make a zigzag or row of dots. For a fancier decoration, squeeze about a teaspoon of sauce onto the plate and, using the back of a spoon, drag the sauce along a 2 to 4 inch curve and release.

Holiday Trifle

My dad loves chocolate. If a dessert doesn't have at least three types of chocolate in it, my dad won't have it. However, this chocolate-free trifle is the sole exception. He goes nuts for the sweet-tart-crunchy-creamy combo and requests it around the holidays every year. Try making this for your most chocolate-dedicated friends and watch them gobble it up.

FILLING

8 ounces cranberries, fresh or frozen
    (about 2½ cups)
½ cup pure maple syrup
¼ cup orange juice

½ teaspoon ground cinnamon
¼ teaspoon ground ginger
Pinch salt
1 teaspoon pure vanilla extract

2 cups store-bought vegan gingersnaps,
    graham crackers, or vanilla wafer
    cookies*

Vanilla Pastry Crème (page 235)

To make the filling: In a medium saucepan, stir together cranberries, maple syrup, orange juice, cinnamon, ginger, and salt. Bring to a boil over medium-high heat. Reduce heat and let simmer, stirring frequently, for about 15 minutes, or until cranberries begin to pop and turn saucy. Remove from heat, mix in vanilla, and add more maple syrup to taste.

To assemble the parfaits: Pulse cookies in a food processor until they are coarse crumbs. Layer a couple spoonfuls of cranberry filling, cookie crumbs, and pastry crème in cocktail or parfait glasses until filled to the top.

*For a gluten-free alternative, substitute gluten-free cookies and see page 11.

Drink Up!

Nuts for Hot Cocoa

SERVES 2

A tablespoon of nut butter is the secret ingredient in this thick and creamy hot cocoa. Cozy up with a mug of it, and poof! Rainy day blues, be gone!

2 cups soy, almond, or rice milk
½ cup semisweet chocolate chips (dairy-free)

1 tablespoon creamy almond or peanut butter
1 tablespoon sugar

In a medium saucepan, combine all ingredients. Heat over medium, stirring frequently, until the chocolate has melted and the mixture is smooth. Remove from heat and serve.

Piña Colada

If you like piña coladas . . . then you will love this easy dairy-free recipe! My dad would blend these up (virgin, of course!) at all my childhood birthday parties. I don't know what my friends liked more: the actual drink or the fact that it was served to them with a cocktail umbrella and pineapple wedge.

1 pint coconut sorbet

1 cup pineapple juice

1 cup ice

4 to 6 tablespoons rum, optional

In a blender, combine coconut sorbet and pineapple juice. Blend until smooth. Add ice, and blend again until smooth. Add more pineapple juice, if needed. Blend in rum, if using, 1 tablespoon at a time, to taste. Pour into glasses and serve immediately.

Pumpkin Spice Latte

SERVES 2 TO 3

Skip the long coffee lines and whip up your own holiday beverage. This Pumpkin Spice Latte, or "liquid pumpkin pie," as I like to call it, will warm your tummy and soul with aromatic pumpkin goodness. If you are making this for kids, omit the espresso.

1 cup soy, almond, or rice milk
¾ cup water
¾ cup pumpkin puree, canned or
    cooked fresh
¼ cup sugar

2 teaspoons instant espresso powder
1 teaspoon pumpkin pie spice
¼ teaspoon salt
Coconut Whipped Cream (page 234),
    optional

In a medium saucepan, whisk together all ingredients. Heat over medium heat, whisking frequently, until the mixture comes to a simmer. Remove from heat and serve with Coconut Whipped Cream, if desired.

It's a Date! Shake

SERVES 2 TO 3

Dates are rich in fiber, potassium, and vitamins, and are also excellent for sweetening and thickening milkshakes. I use Medjools because they are the largest and sweetest variety. If you love dates like I do, make your shake extra chunky and eat it with a spoon. Now, that's my idea of a perfect date!

¼ cup soy, rice, or almond milk
1 pint dairy-free vanilla ice cream

1 cup ice
8 Medjool dates, pitted

In a blender, combine nondairy milk and ice cream. Blend until smooth. Add more nondairy milk, if needed. Add ice and blend again until smooth. Add dates and blend until dates are incorporated, leaving some chunky pieces remaining. Pour into glasses and serve immediately.

Chocolate Raspberry Shake

SERVES 2

This is the best milkshake flavor combo that has ever existed. One slurp of this, and you will never go back to plain ol' chocolate shakes again!

¾ cup soy, almond, or rice milk
1 cup frozen raspberries

1 pint dairy-free chocolate ice cream

In a blender, combine all ingredients. Blend until smooth. Add more nondairy milk, if needed. Pour into glasses and serve immediately.

Frozen Mocha Latte

SERVES 3

Who needs overpriced blended coffee beverages when you can make your own natural version? Save money and calories as you enjoy this rich and refreshing dairy-free latte!

1 cup soy, almond, or rice milk
1 tablespoon instant espresso powder
1 teaspoon unsweetened cocoa powder
2 tablespoons agave
3 tablespoons Kahlúa, optional

2 cups ice
Coconut Whipped Cream (page 234), optional
Chocolate Sauce (page 232), optional

In a blender, combine nondairy milk, espresso powder, cocoa, agave, and Kahlúa, if using. Blend until smooth. Add ice, and blend again until smooth. Taste, and add more espresso powder if a stronger coffee flavor desired. For more sweetness, add more agave. Pour into glasses and serve immediately. Top with Coconut Whipped Cream and Chocolate Sauce, if desired.

Blackberry Margarita

SERVES 4

Margarita makeover! Say adiós *to syrupy sweet slushes with artificial colors, and* hola *to this naturally sweetened antioxidant-rich cocktail.* Qué rica!

2 cups frozen blackberries
½ cup tequila
½ cup agave

¼ cup orange juice
¼ cup lime juice
3 cups ice

In a blender, combine blackberries, tequila, agave, orange juice, and lime juice. Blend until smooth. Add ice, and blend again until smooth. Pour into glasses and serve immediately.

Peanut Butter Chocolate Chip Milkshake

SERVES 2

My brother Andy goes nuts for these milkshakes and can pretty much drink the whole pitcher in one gulp. The ground chocolate chip bits add texture and richness that any chocolate lover will appreciate.

½ cup soy, almond, or rice milk
½ cup creamy peanut butter
1 pint dairy-free vanilla ice cream

1 cup ice
½ cup semisweet chocolate chips
   (dairy-free)

In a blender, combine nondairy milk, peanut butter, and ice cream. Blend until smooth. Add more nondairy milk, if needed. Add ice, and blend again until smooth. Add chocolate chips and blend until chips are finely chopped. Pour into glasses and serve immediately.

Vodka Basil Lemonade

This Italian-style lemonade is fragrant, refreshing, and agave sweetened. It may seem strange to infuse basil in lemonade, but the flavor combo really works. If you're serving kids, omit the vodka. I often bottle this up and take it as a hostess gift to dinner or cocktail parties, and it's always a huge hit! One friend even begged me not to reveal the recipe in this book because he thought I should package and sell it. Oh well—enjoy the recipe!

Make-Ahead Tip:

Basil lemonade can be made in advanced and stored in the refrigerator for up to 2 days. Stir in vodka before serving.

1 4-ounce bunch fresh basil, rinsed and roots removed

1¼ cups light agave or 2 cups sugar

7 cups water, divided, plus more to taste

2 cups lemon juice (about 12 medium lemons)

1 cup vodka, optional

Reserve some basil leaves for garnish. In a medium saucepan, combine basil, agave or sugar, and 1 cup water. Bring to a boil, and then reduce heat and let simmer for 5 minutes, stirring frequently. Remove from heat, strain liquid into a pitcher, and discard basil. Let cool completely. Stir in lemon juice and remaining 6 cups water. Taste, and add more water if needed. If using, add vodka to taste. Chill and serve over ice with basil garnish.

Peach Bellini

SERVES 6

When my mom and I threw a bridal shower for our friend Brooke, we called these Italian cocktails "Brooke's Bellinis." All the ladies loved them and it certainly got our luncheon off to a bubbly start. Much lighter and way more fun than the expected mimosa!

1 cup peach nectar

1 bottle chilled Prosecco or other sparkling wine

Pour 3 tablespoons peach nectar into each glass. Fill the rest of each glass with approximately ⅓ cup Prosecco.

Basics

Chocolate Sauce

MAKES ABOUT 1½ CUPS

Drizzle this chocolate sauce on pretty much any dessert in the book: milkshakes, cupcakes, ice cream, you name it!

Make-Ahead Tip:
Can be made up to 5 days in advance and stored in the refrigerator. Reheat before serving.

½ cup soy, almond, or rice milk
1 teaspoon instant espresso powder

1 cup semisweet chocolate chips
 (dairy-free)
2 teaspoons canola oil

In a small saucepot over medium heat, whisk nondairy milk and espresso powder until combined. Turn the heat to low and mix in chocolate chips until melted and smooth. Remove from heat and stir in oil.

Raspberry Sauce

Add some color to any dessert with this bright and beautiful raspberry sauce. You can also use it to write "Happy Birthday" on a plate!

Make-Ahead Tip:
Can be made up to 5 days in advance and stored in the refrigerator.

1 (12-ounce) bag frozen raspberries or 2 cups fresh raspberries	¼ cup sugar
	⅛ teaspoon salt
2 tablespoons water	1 teaspoon lemon juice

In a medium saucepan, cook raspberries, water, sugar, and salt over medium heat for about 15 minutes, or until thick and saucy. Remove from heat and stir in lemon juice. Add the sauce to a blender, and blend until smooth. For a smoother sauce, press through a fine-mesh strainer to remove the seeds. Let cool, then store in refrigerator.

Coconut Whipped Cream

MAKES ABOUT 1½ CUPS

Vegan whipped cream is possible! Coconut milk is a fabulous, natural substitute for heavy cream.

Note: For best results, Coconut Whipped Cream should chill in the refrigerator for 3 hours or overnight before serving.

1 (13.5-ounce) can of coconut milk (not lite), preferably Thai Kitchen brand or Whole Foods 365 brand, chilled, not stirred

⅔ cup powdered sugar

Chill the bowl and whisk of a stand mixer in the freezer for about 10 minutes. If they are not very cold, the cream will not whip properly. Skim the solidified coconut cream from the chilled can of coconut milk and transfer the solids to the bowl of the stand mixer. Do not include any of the coconut water, even if you have to leave behind a little margin of coconut cream (even a little bit of coconut water can harm your results).

Add the powdered sugar and whip for a few minutes until the mixture begins to stiffen and turn into whipped cream. Chill the whipped cream in a covered container in the refrigerator. It should firm up even more as it sits in the refrigerator for the next few hours or overnight.

Chloe's Tip: Work Quickly

The colder your kitchen and equipment are, the better your whipped cream will hold up. Work quickly to keep everything cool.

Vanilla Pastry Crème

MAKES ABOUT 2 CUPS

This vegan recipe for pastry crème is every bit as smooth and creamy as traditional European pastry crème.

Note: The Vanilla Pastry Crème will need to chill in the refrigerator for 3 hours or overnight.

¼ cup soy, almond, or rice milk
¼ cup cornstarch or arrowroot
1 (13.5-ounce) can coconut milk

½ cup sugar
⅛ teaspoon salt
1 teaspoon pure vanilla extract

In a small bowl, thoroughly mix nondairy milk and cornstarch with a whisk or fork and set aside.

In a medium saucepan, whisk together coconut milk, sugar, and salt, and heat over medium-high heat just until boiling. Reduce the heat to medium and slowly drizzle the cornstarch mixture into the saucepan, whisking continuously. Let cook until the mixture becomes very thick in texture, like pudding, about 5 minutes, whisking frequently. Remove from heat, whisk in vanilla, and transfer to a bowl. Cover with plastic wrap, pressing the surface of the pastry crème with the plastic wrap to prevent a skin from forming. Let cool slightly, then chill in the refrigerator until cool to the touch, about 3 hours or overnight. If the pastry creme gets too firm, process it in a food processor, in batches, until smooth.

Crème Anglaise

Crème Anglaise is a French pouring custard used to top desserts or eaten on its own. My dairy- and sugar-free version is every bit as creamy and comes together in seconds. Spoon this not-too-sweet dessert topping over cake or fresh fruit.

Note: The Crème Anglaise will need to chill in the refrigerator for 3 hours or overnight before serving.

1½ cups canned coconut milk, mixed
    well before measuring
1 cup raw cashews*
⅓ cup maple syrup

1 teaspoon pure vanilla extract
⅛ teaspoon salt
3 tablespoons canola or coconut oil

In a blender, combine coconut milk, cashews, maple syrup, vanilla, and salt, and blend until smooth. Add oil and blend again. Chill in the refrigerator for 3 hours or overnight.

*If you are not using a high-powered blender, such as a Vitamix, soak the cashews overnight or boil for 10 minutes and drain. This will soften the cashews and ensure a silky smooth cream.

Vanilla Ice Cream

Turn any dessert à la mode with a scoop of homemade Vanilla Ice Cream.

1 (13.5-ounce) can coconut milk
1½ cups almond or soy milk
¾ cup agave
3 tablespoons canola oil

1 teaspoon pure vanilla extract
⅛ teaspoon salt
¾ teaspoon xanthan or guar gum

Process coconut milk, almond milk, agave, oil, vanilla, salt, and xanthan gum in a blender. Chill in the refrigerator for 3 hours. Once the ice cream base is chilled, prepare in an ice cream maker according to manufacturer's instructions.

Cookie Icing

Use this as an icing base for any cookie that needs dressing up. Feel free to add food coloring or sprinkle it with edible decorations to jazz it up.

⅓ cup vegan margarine, melted

3 cups powdered sugar

4 to 5 tablespoons water

Natural food coloring, optional

In a medium bowl, whisk margarine and powdered sugar. Add water, 1 tablespoon at a time, until it reaches a smooth icing consistency. Whisk in a few drops of food coloring, if using.

Vanilla Frosting

This is my go-to vanilla frosting, which can be used as a base for just about any flavor. If preferred, substitute refined coconut oil for the shortening.

Make-Ahead Tip:

Can be stored in the refrigerator for up to 2 weeks. Thaw and beat with a stand or hand mixer, if necessary, before frosting.

- 1 cup non-hydrogenated vegetable shortening
- 3 cups powdered sugar
- 1 teaspoon pure vanilla extract
- 3 to 5 tablespoons soy, almond, or rice milk

Using a stand or hand mixer, beat shortening until smooth. With the mixer running on low, add powdered sugar, vanilla, and 1 tablespoon nondairy milk at a time, as needed, until frosting reaches a spreadable consistency. Increase the speed to high and beat for 2 more minutes, until light and fluffy.

Fudge Frosting

This frosting is the real deal: dark, rich, and decadent. If preferred, substitute refined coconut oil for the vegan magarine.

4 ounces unsweetened chocolate	1 teaspoon pure vanilla extract
½ cup vegan margarine	5 tablespoons soy, almond,
4 cups powdered sugar	or rice milk

Melt chocolate and margarine over medium-low heat in a small saucepan. Whisk until smooth.

Using a stand or hand mixer, beat the melted chocolate mixture, powdered sugar, vanilla, and nondairy milk until smooth and spreadable. If needed, add more nondairy milk, a little at a time. Apply frosting immediately to cake or cupcakes before it sets.

Single Piecrust

This simple vegan recipe is a great alternative to store-bought piecrust.

1¼ cups all-purpose flour (or half all-purpose flour and half whole-wheat pastry flour), plus extra for rolling
1½ teaspoons sugar
½ teaspoon salt

½ cup non-hydrogenated vegetable shortening or vegan margarine (if using margarine, omit salt)
5 tablespoons ice-cold water, as needed

You can make the dough by hand or using a food processor.

By hand: In a medium bowl, whisk together flour, sugar, and salt. Using a pastry cutter, cut shortening into flour until mixture has a crumbly consistency. Add ice water, 1 tablespoon at a time, and mix with a spoon until the dough just holds together. You may not need to use all the water. Do not overwork.

Using a food processor: Add flour, sugar, and salt to the food processor. Pulse until ingredients are combined. Add shortening and pulse until mixture has a crumbly consistency. Add ice water, 1 tablespoon at a time, and pulse until the dough just holds together. You may not need to use all the water. Do not overprocess.

Form the dough into a disc and wrap in plastic wrap. Store in the refrigerator until ready to use. If the dough is difficult to roll, let it soften at room temperature until it is easier to work with.

Double Piecrust

MAKES TWO 9-INCH PIECRUSTS

2½ cups all-purpose flour (or half all-purpose flour and half whole-wheat pastry flour), plus extra for rolling

1 tablespoon sugar

1 teaspoon salt

1 cup non-hydrogenated vegetable shortening or vegan margarine (if using margarine, omit salt)

10 tablespoons ice-cold water, as needed

You can make the dough by hand or using a food processor.

By hand: In a medium bowl, whisk together flour, sugar, and salt. Using a pastry cutter, cut shortening into flour until mixture has a crumbly consistency. Add ice water, 1 tablespoon at a time, and mix with a wooden spoon until the dough just holds together. You may not need to use all of the water. Do not overwork.

Using a food processor: Add flour, sugar, and salt to the food processor. Pulse until ingredients are combined. Add shortening and pulse until mixture has a crumbly consistency. Add ice water, 1 tablespoon at a time, and pulse until the dough just holds together. You may not need to use all of the water. Do not overprocess.

Form the dough into 2 discs and wrap in plastic wrap. Store in the refrigerator until ready to use. If the dough is difficult to roll, let it soften at room temperature until it is easier to work with.

Gluten-Free Piecrust

This simple no-roll crust is a great gluten-free alternative. Feel free to use this in place of traditional piecrust in any pie or tart recipe. Sometimes I even like to bake this, break it up into pieces, and eat them like cookies, because this crust is so flavorful and delicious! Whether or not you're gluten-free, this crust is a great way to spice up your favorite pie.

½ cup rolled oats
½ cup almonds
¾ cup oat flour
¼ teaspoon ground cinnamon

⅛ teaspoon salt
¼ cup maple syrup or agave
¼ cup canola oil

Preheat the oven to 350 degrees. Lightly grease a 9-inch pie pan.

In a food processor, combine oats, almonds, oat flour, cinnamon, and salt. Process until a fine meal forms. Add maple syrup and oil, and pulse until mixture comes together. The mixture will be wet. Press firmly into the prepared pan, working the dough evenly up the sides of the pan with your fingertips.

Bake piecrust for 15 to 20 minutes, or until lightly browned around the edges and set in the center.

Toasted Coconut

Here is my easy method for toasting coconut. It will keep in the freezer for months, so I like to make it in large batches.

Shredded coconut

Preheat oven to 350 degrees. Spread coconut on a rimmed baking sheet and bake for 5 to 10 minutes, or until golden. Turn coconut with a spatula frequently to ensure even browning.

Toasted Nuts

Toasting nuts sounds simple, but many people do not know how to do it properly. Here's how.

Spread the nuts in one layer on a rimmed baking sheet and bake at 350 degrees for about 8 to 12 minutes, until lightly browned and fragrant. Transfer nuts to a bowl; they will continue to cook a bit after you remove them from the heat.

Chloe's Tip: Set a timer

I usually have a good sense of time when I'm baking cakes or cookies, but there is something about toasting nuts that gets even the best of chefs. Trust me, set the timer. Toasting nuts can be a forgettable task, and you don't want the smell of burnt almonds to be your reminder!

Acknowledgments

Writing a dessert cookbook is no piece of cake, but having an incredible, passionate team makes the process much sweeter. A heartfelt thank you to everyone at Atria, Simon & Schuster who made this book possible: my brilliant editors Leslie Meredith and Dominick Anfuso; publicists extraordinaire Carisa Hays, Meg Cassidy, and Meagan Brown; and Donna Loffredo, Martha Levin, Suzanne Donahue, Jackie Jou, Nicole Judge, Erich Hobbing, Phil Metcalf, and Eric Fuentecilla. I believe that we eat with our eyes first, so this book would not nearly be as delicious without my talented and creative photographers, Miki Duisterhof, Teri Lyn Fisher, and Robert Raphael. I would also like to thank Heike Grebenstein of hgfinejewelry.com, *VegNews* magazine, Natural Gourmet Institute, Eric Lupfer, Aaron Lea, Sheri Terry, Nan Whitney, Mariana Velasquez, Steven Boljonis, Tiffany Howe, Lisa Bloom, CJ Yu, Linda Wolvek, Anna Bolek, Taylor Rowley, Ava E. Naimi, Sonia Sohaili, Monica Malaviya, Sandhya Jacob, Susan Welsh, Chef Elliott Prag, Rosemary Serviss, and my talented team of recipe testers: Stephanie Kivich, Ann Marie Monteiro, Frida Kristinsdottir, Nancy Sobel, Stephanie Puno, and Tim Ferrell. Hugs and kisses to my amazing family, Mommy, Daddy, and Andy, for supporting me and taste testing every recipe in the book. What would I do without you? There's only so much chocolate one girl can eat!

Most importantly, thank *you!* I am overjoyed that my book has made it into your hands and my desserts onto your table.

Index

Page numbers in *italics* refer to illustrations.

About the Author

Chef Chloe Coscarelli is a Food Network–winning vegan chef and author of *Chloe's Kitchen: 125 Easy Delicious Recipes for Making the Food You Love the Vegan Way,* proving to the world that vegan food can be stylish, delicious, and easy. She took home first place in the Food Network's *Cupcake Wars,* making her the first vegan ever to win a Food Network competition. Chloe is a graduate of The Natural Gourmet Institute of Health and Culinary Arts NYC and the University of California, Berkeley, as well as of Cornell University's Plant Based Nutrition Program by Dr. T. Colin Campbell (The China Study). Additional work includes Millennium Restaurant San Francisco, Counter Organic Vegetarian Bistro New York City, and Herbivore Restaurant Berkeley.